Farrakhan and Education

SECOND EDITION

By Abul Pitre

Bassim Hamadeh, CEO and Publisher
Kassie Graves, Director of Acquisitions and Sales
Jamie Giganti, Senior Managing Editor
Miguel Macias, Senior Graphic Designer
Zina Craft, Senior Field Acquisitions Editor
Alisa Munoz, Licensing Coordinator
Kaela Martin, Associate Editor
Abbey Hastings, Associate Production Editor

Copyright © 2018 by Abul Pitre. All rights reserved. No part of this publication may be reprinted, reproduced, transmitted, or utilized in any form or by any electronic, mechanical, or other means, now known or hereafter invented, including photocopying, microfilming, and recording, or in any information retrieval system without the written permission of Cognella, Inc. For inquiries regarding permissions, translations, foreign rights, audio rights, and any other forms of reproduction, please contact the Cognella Licensing Department at rights@cognella.com.

Trademark Notice: Product or corporate names may be trademarks or registered trademarks, and are used only for identification and explanation without intent to infringe.

Cover image copyright: "Farrakhan," https://en.wikipedia.org/wiki/File:Farrakhan.jpg.
Copyright in the Public Domain.
Copyright © Depositphotos/michaeljung.
Copyright © Depositphotos/titoOnz.

Printed in the United States of America

ISBN: 978-1-5165-0655-1 (pb) / 978-1-5165-0666-8 (br)

*Dedicated to my grandmother (Mother)
who has shaped me for THEM.*

Contents

Praise for Farrakhan and Education   vii
Preface   ix
Introduction   xiii

Chapter 1: The Roots of Farrakhan's Educational Philosophy   1
Chapter 2: The Prophetic Voice in Transforming Education   11
Chapter 3: Determining the Purpose of Education   25
Chapter 4: Farrakhan and the Human Development
           Approach to Education   39
Chapter 5: Critical Pedagogy   53

Conclusion: Is There Room in Educational Theory
           for Louis Farrakhan?   73

References   77
About the Author   83
Index   85

Praise for Farrakhan and Education

"Abul Pitre's *Farrakhan and Education* is an eye-opening study of the educational ideas of a very humble man who has sacrificed his life in the cause of *freedom*, *justice*, and *equality* for oppressed people. The book represents a paradigm shift that will reshape education in the 21st century. It clearly shows that Farrakhan received a torch (*knowledge emanating*) from Elijah Muhammad and now society awaits the next leader that will receive the torch (*knowledge emanating*) from Louis Farrakhan to educate the whole of humanity. This is a *must read* for anyone wanting to learn more about the historical journey of Louis Farrakhan, the Honorable Elijah Muhammad, and the Nation of Islam and their ideas about education."

—*Belinda K. Collins, doctoral candidate, Prairie View A&M University*

"Pitre offers an instructive yet critical analysis of an alternate approach to education, with emphasis on African Americans. Embedded in the social political philosophy of the Honorable Elijah Muhammad, Minister Louis Farrakhan advances a Black perspective, in the process of describing and evaluating the Africana experience in regards to the humanities, social sciences, and professions."

—*James Conyers, director of African American Studies, University of Houston*

Preface

With so much negative media attention about Louis Farrakhan in recent years, one may well ask why anyone would want to undertake a study on such a figure, especially as the media has done an excellent job of portraying him as antithetical to any decent, civilized way of life. News media declare him to be divisive, anti-Christian, and even anti-American. Sadly, even those concerned with scholarship have been unwilling to investigate the positive attributes that have made him influential for so many people.

This book departs from previous social science related perspectives to delve into Farrakhan's educational ideas. The reader will find that Louis Farrakhan has articulated a critique of education that aligns with critical educational theory. Derrick Bell (1992), one of the founders of critical race theory, wrote that he is "smart and superarticulate" (p.118).

And achievements—from his resurrection of the Nation of Islam and his work in the Black community—made him deeply invested in the educational journey of Black children. His reflections on the educational process has echoed and sometimes even preceded those of the great educational thinkers, resulting in a true educational paradigm shift (Kuhn, 1962), a revolution in the thinking process about what education accomplishes and how it does so.

The shadow cast over the legacy of Louis Farrakhan has made it almost impossible for scholars to approach his thought in a more objective, open-minded manner. My own approach to Farrakhan evolved over many years as I completed my doctoral studies and began to teach. Between completing my doctorate and starting to work in a very unique urban education program, I began to see the dynamic intersectionality of critical educational scholarship to the teachings of Elijah Muhammad, and this study of Elijah Muhammad brought me into contact with the educational ideas of Louis Farrakhan.

Over time my exposure to his thinking increased. In 2007, I was invited to the Nation of Islam's Savior's Day convention to sit on an education panel where my book *The Educational Philosophy of Elijah Muhammad: Education for a New World* was introduced. A few months after the convention I was invited to attend an educational conference that was convened by Minister Farrakhan. And in 2009, Louis Farrakhan released *The Education Challenge: The New Educational Paradigm*. These events began to synchronize, causing me to take an intimate study of Louis Farrakhan in the context of educational theory.

Reflecting on this study of Louis Farrakhan has made it abundantly clear how difficult it is for scholars on the periphery to understand his body of work. News commentaries and media portrayals have muddied his image in a way that makes it virtually impossible for the lay person or scholar to truly understand his contributions. A good example of this muddying was the 2008 presidential debate at the University of Texas, when the late Tim Russell queried presidential hopeful Barack Obama about Farrakhan's purported support of his candidacy.

The question seemed to shock Obama; after some chiding, he distanced himself from Farrakhan and was rewarded with an array of cheers from a mostly White audience. Farrakhan himself noted that he is the litmus test for Blacks aspiring to privileged positions. Law professor Derrick Bell described the Farrakhan litmus test this way: "When a black person or group makes a statement or takes an action that the white community or vocal components thereof deem 'outrageous' the latter will actively recruit blacks willing to refute the statement or condemn the action" (Bell, 1992, p. 118). Likewise, in academia, any positive discussion about Farrakhan could mean death to one's career status.

In the pages of this book, you will come across what I hope is an antidote to such unthinking responses. This volume is intended to comparatively analyze Farrakhan's educational ideas with those of other scholars in the areas of Afrocentric education, multicultural education, and critical pedagogy.

What develops from these areas is a *critical black pedagogy in education,* or the study of Black leaders and their work to challenge the unjust schooling and educational experiences of Blacks in America. At this juncture in world history, critical Black pedagogy in education is crucial to see beyond the mirage of equity and equality of education to devise a just and practical resolution to the crises of educating Black and other historically underserved groups.

The human suffering that is now taking center stage in our interdependent world should compel educators to reexamine the way we educate and have been educated. It should inspire us to look to a *higher education* that will bring forth excellence in the human being. This volume is a beginning point for exploring that higher education, by way of Louis Farrakhan, releasing him from the prison walls that have denied us access to a fellow comrade in the human struggle for freedom, justice, and equality for the whole of humanity.

Introduction

In his newly released study guide, *The Education Challenge: A New Educational Paradigm for the 21st Century*, Minister Louis Farrakhan lays the foundation for deeper study into the field of education and its significance in bringing to birth an educational paradigm shift that will produce a new world. He writes, "This is telling us the type of thing we are and must be engaged in, which is to stimulate or challenge our intellect over the problem that is found in education" (2009, p. 11).

Shifting the paradigm in education is indeed a daunting task, problematic because of the historical structuring that has fueled the cultural experiences of the masses living in worlds and systems that are tied to the educational system. If we define education as "leading out" or "bringing forth" the attributes intrinsic to human beings for the greater good of the system or organization, then education has served the interest of the powerful.

Dr. Muhammad Yunus illustrates the impact of systems on the development of culture, attitudes, and dispositions when he describes the current capitalist system as striving on the idea of profit. Yunus (2007) argues that profit caters to the more selfish characteristics of the individual, leaving the most humane parts of our nature undernourished. He proposes that we look at new systems, one of which he refers to as *social business*. Unlike organizations enmeshed in profit business, which are built on *taking*, Yunus's ideal system of social business is based on the principle of *giving*.

This type of system undermines the current educational and organizational systems that work in the interest of producing "things" rather than authentic human beings (Freire, 2000). *Giving* is the most basic principle of so many of our world religions. Matthew 25 illustrates this when Jesus' followers ask, "Lord, when did we ever see you hungry and feed you? Or thirsty and give you something to drink?" and Jesus responds that as his followers did to "the least of these my brothers and sisters," they did to him also (New Living Translation). We cannot have a humane world if our business and education and entire psychology are oriented toward taking rather than giving.

At the core of the American educational system is the corporate capitalist interest in getting an ample supply of workers whose labor can be used in the interest of the ruling elite. The corporate capitalist interest in education has resulted in an educational system that is developed along tiers, each housing the roles that individuals will play within the system (Bowles, 2012). A select group of students receives an education that makes them leaders and producers, while the masses of students receive an education that makes them followers and consumers.

Jean Anyon (1980) describes these differing schools in her article "Social Class and the Hidden Curriculum of Work," naming four different types of schools: working class, middle class, affluent, and executive elite. For Anyon, these schools' curricula reflect the future roles students are expected to assume once their educations are complete. Farrakhan (2009) summarizes the tiers this way: "You have an educational system that has an elite at the top, then a lesser elite and a lesser elite, then the mass who work for the elite" (p. 17). This system—one that produces workers for corporate capitalist interest—has been called *mis-education* (Chomsky, 2000; Woodson, 1999).

America's educational system, like all systems, is rooted in rules of discourse, language, artifacts, and symbols that are imbedded into disciplines or fields of studies. All systems employ language and symbols to convey how ideas should be looked at and which people or events are considered important, and our current educational system is grounded in European theoretical constructs. For example,

John Dewey is considered a major philosophical figure, an icon of educational philosophy, but other figures such as Carter G. Woodson are nearly entirely omitted from the curricula. Woodson was a distinguished educator in the early twentieth century and one of the first historians to study African American history specifically, founding the *Journal of Negro History* in 1915.

Yet in a recent conversation, a group of students in a doctoral-level education course disclosed they never heard of Carter G. Woodson, despite his seminal work on Black education and the numerous schools named after him across the country. This is an example of the problematic nature of our current paradigm: the rules, language, symbols, artifacts, and discourse of education have been built by Europeans and continue to dominate the educational landscape.

This domination, which lionizes some figures and discards others, is a form of White supremacy so invisible that it gives the impression that education is neutral, without political implications. It also gives birth to hegemony—consent by the oppressed to be dominated by those who rule. Educators almost unthinkingly view the problem of education and society from the perspective of the ruling elite, which sees the oppressed "as marginal persons who deviate from the general configuration of a 'good, organized, and just' society" (Freire, 2000, p. 24).

Watkins (2001a) confirms this hegemony: "Organized education, much like organized religion, has long been influenced by the forces of the power structure, the state, and those with an ideological agenda" (p. 10). Any deviation from the current paradigm is seen as disruptive and unproductive, and educators under such a system in turn become oppressors. Educators become witting or unwitting perpetuators of White supremacy; as Louis Farrakhan wrote, "the White man is the god of his own world, and his idea is to make everybody into his own image and after his own likeness" (Farrakhan, 2009, p. 27).

The American education system is stuck in a paradigm that reproduces the thinking and imagery of White supremacy. To effect true change in the educational system, then, it becomes necessary to create a new paradigm. Thomas Kuhn (1962) is credited with shaping the contemporary concept of paradigm. Kuhn's work has been specifically related to the field of science with a focus on the history of science. He explains, "A paradigm is the way we see the world—not in terms of our visual sense of sight, but in terms of perceiving, understanding and interpreting. A paradigm shift is when we take the leap moving from one thought system to another" (cited in Muhammad, 2009, p. 82). Handa (1986) applied this definition to the social sciences and education fields, and Banks (2006) further defines the concept as "an interrelated set of facts, concepts, generalizations, and theories that attempt to explain human behavior or social phenomenon and that imply policy and action" (p. 91).

To shift paradigms, we must change the educational systems that shape our worldview. Shifting educational paradigms is very problematic because it disrupts the prevailing structures that dominate discourse. Pinar et al. (2008) argue, "When a field shifts from one major paradigm to another, many scholars are left with allegiances to concepts that are no longer pertinent" (p. 13). This is an uncomfortable position for many to be in, and resistance is almost inevitable. But it is crucial if we want to allow students to fully develop their talents and capabilities, to grow into their fullest selves.

Such a paradigm shift was one of the great contributions of Elijah Muhammad and Louis Farrakhan. Elijah Muhammad's entire mission was educational, and he emphasized that his teacher, Wallace Fard Muhammad, had studied every educational system in the civilized world—a field that is now called comparative education. According to Elijah Muhammad, Wallace Fard Muhammad was a worldwide traveler, and his international experiences and teachings were preparation for the universal education that he was preparing for the New World.

Elijah Muhammad declared, "What Allah has revealed to me is a base for building universal knowledge. It has not become universal or we would not be preaching. It is to become universal" (Pitre, 2015, p. xviii). Elijah Muhammad advocated education that emanated from multiple sources and individual contemplation rather than from the European model. The paradigm shift had to transform the source of knowledge as well as the content. It also advocated for the downtrodden Blacks of America to seek the knowledge of self, which forms the basis of elite education.

Close your eyes and envision the higher education institutions in America. Think about the major research universities that you see competing every week on television during football and basketball seasons. The football crowds exceed 100,000 at several major research schools—and these crowds are predominantly White. These are the institutions conducting ground-breaking research, dictating policy, and shaping life both nationally and internationally.

The environment of these institutions creates such a different mindset that one can see that they are in their own worlds. The reality, however, is that the knowledge generated in these universities is the lifeblood of the larger society and is in the domain of a majority White population situated in a White supremacist infrastructure. Thus, without a greater degree of knowledge to combat these institutions, the oppressed are facing a seemingly unconquerable power.

This volume, *Farrakhan and Education,* is intended to contribute to a paradigm shift in American education, one that embodies the principles that Elijah Muhammad and Louis Farrakhan spent much of their careers propounding. We must shift the educational paradigm from a human capitalist ideology to one that cultivates the divine essence in students. In addition, we must look anew at the role of Islam in America. Because Christianity is so tightly enmeshed with European culture and even White supremacy, it is important to look at alternate worldviews and religions in order to break the White supremacist mindset of the past.

While there are several major universities in the U.S. that offer Islamic Studies programs and millions of dollars have been donated to educational institutions and centers for Islamic Studies programs, the discourse in some of these programs does not adequately address the impact of Elijah Muhammad and his role in laying a foundation for Islamic Studies in the U.S.

Farrakhan and Education highlights Louis Farrakhan's contribution to the study of education as the basis for developing human potential. Through the lens of critical pedagogy, the book comparatively explores

Louis Farrakhan's critiques of education, particularly as they relate to historically underserved students. In addition, the book explores the foundations of education by exploring such key concepts as human development, nurture vs. nature, and creativity as the goal of education.

The Birthing of Farrakhan and Education

This book is the highlight of a lifelong journey in the pursuit of bringing to birth a new educational paradigm predicated on the principles of freedom, justice, and equality. Prior to studying Farrakhan in the context of education I was introduced to the teachings of Elijah Muhammad in 1994 when Minister Harold Muhammad served as the guest speaker for a Black History Program at the high school where I served as social studies teacher and program coordinator. The controversy that ensued after the Black History Program moved me to study the teachings of Elijah Muhammad.

This study led me to a long career unpacking the serious and innovative educational philosophies that Elijah Muhammad and Louis Farrakhan expounded in their writings and actions. In my first book, I examined the educational philosophy of Elijah Muhammad within the context of critical multicultural education. This book compared the ideas of Elijah Muhammad with those of later teachings in the field of critical theory, focusing on Muhammad's own writings rather than the popular images and portrayals of Muhammad often circulated by the media.

Since the printing of *The Educational Philosophy of Elijah Muhammad* and *An Introduction to Elijah Muhammad Studies,* I have ventured into the study of Louis Farrakhan's teaching as it relates to education. At one point in this journey, I was asked to teach a course on human development, and my preparation for the course only highlighted the similarities between the theoretical constructs in human development and Louis Farrakhan's teachings. It became apparent that these constructs could be a unique addition to the book; in fact, human development is a major focus of the book.

The study of human development examines the life stages that people undergo as they become and un-become, constantly evolving into something new. Minister Farrakhan's words confirmed the importance of transition in human development: "A period of transition is the most difficult period in human development for during periods of transition the life that is in transition is not where it was, and it is not where it is intended to be. So such periods of time are always very dangerous for the life that is in transition" (Muhammad, 2006, p. 37).

I am indebted to Jabril Muhammad's book *Closing the Gap: Inner Views of the Heart, Mind, and Soul of the Honorable Minister Farrakhan* for expanding my understanding of Farrakhan's human development approach to education and also to Eure and Jerome's (1989) book *Farrakhan: Back Where We Belong—Selected Speeches by Minister Louis Farrakhan*. These speeches and the many study guides that Minister Farrakhan wrote were replete with ideas about human development and the importance of it in our approach to education and to progress in general. For example, one study guide, "Self Improvement: The Basis for Community Development," speaks to these issues:

> I have chosen for my subject "Self Improvement: The Basis for Community Development." Now there are many, many, developers who buy land and develop that land into communities, towns, and cities, placing on this land magnificent structures costing hundreds of millions, even billions of dollars. This activity of land development is going on in Phoenix and in cities around this country, and indeed around the Earth. However, to those who spend those hundreds of millions and billions of dollars building structures, unless we build people, unless the human potential of people is developed then man in his underdeveloped state will ultimately destroy magnificent buildings that he has erected, and destroy the cities that he has built because of revolution and war. (Eure and Jerome, 1989, p. 170)

It became apparent to me that Louis Farrakhan's mission was the development of human potential through education. During Farrakhan's decades of studying and teaching he has offered profound insights on education through his lectures and writings in the area. In this volume, I draw from these lectures to comparatively discuss his educational ideas to that of major scholars in the field of education. Emerging from Louis Farrakhan's educational ideas are concepts similar to the tenets espoused in critical multicultural education, critical pedagogy, and the Afrocentric idea in education by Molefi Asante.

While most people acknowledge that knowledge leads to power; it is those who have been the most marginalized, particularly Blacks, who have been deprived of higher bodies of knowledge, thus hindering them from reaching their full human potential. To address the question of human development in the context of the theological the book addresses major concepts found in Elijah Muhammad's *Theology of Time* and Louis Farrakhan's "The Origin of Blackness" (Hakim, 1997b; Farrakhan, 2009). The book challenges educators to think about education as serving either the goal of domestication or the goal of liberation.

Chapter 1 is a biographical sketch of Louis Farrakhan to help the reader understand how he became a prominent world leader. It touches on the unique circumstances of his birth to his first encounter with Malcolm X and Elijah Muhammad. Among the chapter highlights are his early childhood desires to eradicate Black suffering; the challenges he faced as a new member of the Nation of Islam; and his organization of two major marches—the *Million Man March* and *Justice or Else*.

Chapter 2 places Farrakhan's many years of teaching in the context of educational discourse. Drawing from scholars in critical education theory it highlights the contemporary educational challenges and argues that there is a need for teachers to have historical knowledge. In addition, it places the Million Man March in the context of a social movement that could be used to increase the number of Black male teachers. Highlighted throughout the chapter is Farrakhan's educational discourse in the context of spirituality.

Chapter 3 discloses the purpose of education. It explores how the *white architects* of public education developed a system of education for Blacks. It then highlights the contemporary architects of American education that are continuing to shape education based on a human capitalist ideology. The chapter discusses three major philosophical canons—*idealism, realism,* and *pragmatism*. And it concludes with a discussion on the moral and spiritual crisis in education.

Chapter 4 argues that education is the key to human development by comparing Louis Farrakhan's teachings with theoretical constructs found in the human development approach presented by Newman and Newman (2009). The chapter explores nature versus nurture and creativity; and it touches on the role of environment in the context of the nature versus nurture debate that often takes place in educational discourse. The concluding section of this chapter touches on Islam highlighting scholars of multicultural education who have discussed the significance of including Islam in contemporary educational discourse.

Chapter 5 discusses critical pedagogy in relationship to the Nation of Islam's critique of education. This section raises questions around achievement asking: Who is defining achievement? And what does achievement look like for Black students under a white controlled educational system? In critiquing the discourse around achievement, it also highlights the parallels between Farrakhan's critiques to those of critical educational scholars. The book concludes with an epilogue on getting past some of the barriers to incorporating Farrakhan's educational thinking in teacher education.

Chapter 1:
The Roots of Farrakhan's Educational Philosophy

Louis Farrakhan has led the Nation of Islam for nearly four decades and served in leadership roles for over five decades. In 1995, he spearheaded the Million Man March, in which nearly two million Black men participated. In commemoration of the twentieth anniversary of the Million Man March, on October 10, 2015, he led the *Justice Or Else* movement, drawing people from diverse racial, ethnic, and religious groups to Washington, D.C. These defining historical events demonstrate the extraordinary leadership of this controversial and dynamic figure.

However, few know the background that shaped Farrakhan's world view and leadership. Louis Farrakhan's life journey began with the unusual circumstances of his birth. On May 11, 1933, Louis Walcott was born to Sarah Mae Manning, a Caribbean woman from St. Kitts, in Bronx, New York. His father, whom he never knew, was a light-skinned man from Jamaica named Percy Clarke.

When she learned of the pregnancy, and perhaps because she had been romantically involved at the time with both Clarke and another man, Manning attempted unsuccessfully to abort the child. After three such failed attempts, she resorted to prayer. Perhaps this provided her with the calm she needed to brave the emotional storms resulting from the unexpected pregnancy.

When he was three years old, his mother moved him and his brother Alvin to the Roxbury section of Boston, Massachusetts. There, as a boy, he was a member of the St. Cyprian Episcopal Church and was considered a "deeply religious child ... I used to sing in the choir. I carried the cross. I loved the church. It gave me a wonderful beginning" (Person-Lynn, 1996, p. 172).

What is also clear about the young Louis's early upbringing is that his mother was committed to ensuring he would have the best educational experiences. He would later write, "When I think about my childhood, I would say that I was mischievous, and yet I was quiet and reflective. I was an athlete. I was a musician. I was none of that without my wonderful mother. She put the violin in my hands at five years old" (Person-Lynn, 1996, p. 171).

At the age of thirteen, he played with the Boston College Orchestra and the Boston Civic Symphony. A talented violinist, he won the Ted Mack Amateur Hour and was one of the first Blacks to appear on the show. His preferred extracurricular activities were perhaps inspired by attending the prestigious Boston Latin School, the oldest public school in America and alma mater to the likes of Benjamin Franklin, Ralph Waldo Emerson, and Leonard Bernstein (Angelis, 1998). The school was virtually all-White, which made him feel out of place. After a year, he transferred to the more diverse English High, which afforded him the opportunity to befriend students of different races and religious backgrounds.

His encounter with racism in the school setting occurred when his teacher asked what he wanted to become when he grew up: "I said, 'I want to become a doctor because I want to heal people.' She said, 'Oh Louis, if you became a doctor my people would never come to you and your own people wouldn't trust your medical skill. But you play the violin beautifully'" (Muhammad, 2006, p. 340).

He saw this experience as the teacher's way of motivating him towards a nonthreatening career, but nonetheless reflected on his musical talents and assumed that he could use them to "serve humanity by giving them music to uplift their spirit" (p. 341). It is clear that early on, he was deeply concerned about the plight of Black people; in fact, Muhammad (1996) writes that his mother was conscious of the revolutionary ideas of Marcus Garvey and would give Louis and Alvin "the NAACP's Crisis magazine to read about the atrocities Whites committed on Blacks" (p. 12).

The Crisis magazine, the *Afro-American,* the *Pittsburgh Courier,* and the writings of W. E. B. Du Bois featured visual images that pained the young Louis to the point that he began to yearn for ways to relieve Blacks from the suffering and oppression they were experiencing. He was so moved by the images of Blacks suffering that he would often question his Sunday school teachers about why no one was sent to relieve Blacks from their undue hardships. As a member of the St. Cyprians Episcopal Church he questioned the possibility of God sending someone to save his people: "Why, if God had sent a deliverer to an oppressed people in the past, would God have not sent us a deliverer?" (Angelis, 1998, p. 21)

While on a visit to family in New York, eleven-year-old Louis encountered a picture of a Black man on the wall and inquired about the man's identity. He climbed atop a nearby chair to study the man's features. An uncle told him that the pictured man was Marcus Garvey, a man who had come to unite Black people. The young Louis assumed that this was perhaps the deliverer he had been yearning and asked where he could meet this man. When told of Garvey's death, he began to cry.

Louis went on to excel in both academics and athletics. As an outstanding student-athlete, he graduated at the age of sixteen with a track scholarship to North Carolina's Winston Salem Teachers College. The journey to college was his first trip to the South. North Carolina gave him opportunities to witness the virulent racism and oppression that he had heard so much about.

Yet he had deliberately chosen the location, wanting to understand Black suffering firsthand. He later said, "I was intrigued by the suffering of Black people in the South. I told my mother at a very young age that when I grew up, I wanted to go South. I wanted to experience what my brothers and sisters in the South were experiencing" (Person-Lynn, 1996, p. 172).

After two years in Winston Salem he decided to leave the university to find employment closer to his childhood sweetheart and soon-to-be-wife, Betsy Jean, and the couple's newborn child. He had known Betsy Jean, affectionately called Mother Khadijah by members of the Nation of Islam, since early childhood, "I met my wife when she was eight years old, I was eleven. I liked her then, but I didn't know how strong this like was going to become…By the time she was seventeen and I was twenty, we were married" (Person-Lynn, 1996, p. 180).

After dropping out of college, he pursued a career in music and enjoyed moderate success, eventually producing several albums that earned him the nickname "the Charmer." But unbeknownst to him, the up-and-coming entertainer was destined for an introduction to the Nation of Islam.

In 1953, while in Boston playing a nightclub gig, he shook hands with a young man named Malcolm X who had been preaching in a venue across the street. Like most people who have been fed erroneous information about the Nation of Islam, he didn't want to be involved with "anybody who had a message or doctrine that preached hate" (Person-Lynn, p. 173); after meeting Malcolm X, he "shook his hand and quickly moved away from him" (p. 173).

Then in 1955, while playing at a nightclub in Chicago, a Muslim friend invited him to Savior's Day, the Nation of Islam's annual birthday celebration for its founder, Wallace Fard Muhammad. From his balcony seat, he took in a lecture given by Elijah Muhammad—and he was less than impressed with the latter's delivery:

> I, being a student of English, and verb and subject agreement, heard him speak in a manner that a public speaker who was familiar with English wouldn't do. So in my head I said, "Oh, this man can't even talk." When I said that he looked right at me and said, Brother, I didn't get a chance to get that fine education that you got. When I got to the school the doors was closed. Don't pay any attention to how I'm saying it. You pay attention to what I'm saying and then you take it and put it in that fine language that you know. As I said, I was a little frightened because he seemed to know

1. The Roots of Farrakhan's Educational Philosophy

what I was thinking. But looking back I see that he literally gave me my assignment the first day that he laid eyes on me. (Muhammad, 2009, pp. 26–27)

This lecture piqued his interest in the Nation of Islam, and he began to attend the mosque where Malcolm X was minister, and the two began a relationship similar to that of father and son, "He was, to me, like the father I never had. He became my tutor, my mentor, my instructor in the principles of Islam, in the teachings of the Honorable Elijah Muhammad, and the disciplined life of a Muslim" (Person-Lynn, 1996, p. 173).

The early years of his conversion were beset with difficult choices that seem to afflict most converts to the Nation of Islam. In his 2006 historical book, *Closing the Gap: Inner Views of the Heart, Mind and Soul of the Honorable Minister Louis Farrakhan*, Jabril Muhammad discloses these difficulties, some of which were severe.

One particular challenge was that he already had a promising career as an entertainer. The money he was garnering for his musical talents was supporting his young family. But Elijah Muhammad had issued an ultimatum demanding that all members of the Nation of Islam who were involved in show business leave the industry within thirty days.

Determining that he could not live without truth, he gave up show business, sacrificing the $500 he had been earning weekly as a musician. Instead he worked odd jobs washing dishes, mopping floors, and taking orders for coffee and doughnuts, but was unsuccessful in each position. Nonetheless, he persevered: "I failed at pretty much every day jobs that I had but I was determined that I wasn't going backward" (Muhammad, 2006, p. 349).

The next trial, brought on by his inability to keep a job for a sustained period, was poverty. The minister later called it a trial of extreme poverty and described how he and his wife Khadijah would take "shopping bags and go down and pick up food out of the street to fill our shopping bag and come back and feed our growing family" (Muhammad, 2006, p. 352). The energy needed to sustain the new convert during these trying times may have come from his 1957 experience with Elijah Muhammad.

In 1957, as captain of the Boston Mosque, he had a chance to dine with Elijah Muhammad. He later recalled an experience during dinner that perhaps prepared him for his future mission: "At the end of the dinner he [Elijah Muhammad] went around the table shaking everybody's hand. When he got to me and shook my hand he came close and whispered in my ear; you remind me of David" (Muhammad, 2006, p. 350). These powerful words may have given Farrakhan hope that his future would one day change for the better.

Another trial came when Malcolm X split from Elijah Muhammad. After the assassination of President Kennedy, Elijah Muhammad forbade his ministers to comment on the tragedy. He believed even the most innocuous of statements could be blown out of proportion and result in another attack on the Nation of Islam. However, during an interview in which Malcolm X was asked for his thoughts on the assassination, he responded, "the chickens have come home to roost" (Person-Lynn, 1996, p. 174). The media used the quote to portray the Nation of Islam as being unsympathetic to the tragic event, and for his misstep, Elijah Muhammad suspended Malcolm for ninety days.

Minister Farrakhan noted that while this silencing of Malcolm X could be construed as severe, it was in reality a safeguard that may have thwarted an attempt on Malcolm's life, "You may not believe this, but it is true: he did it as much for Malcolm as he did it for the Nation. If Malcolm had continued to speak during that time, he might have been assassinated then" (Person-Lynn, 1996, p. 174).

During those ninety days, with agents placed in the Nation of Islam and perhaps jealous members within the Nation of Islam, Malcolm X began to speak negatively of his teacher. Combined with fabrications and misquotes, this drove a bigger wedge between the two, and to his dismay Farrakhan was faced with the dilemma of choosing between them. He decided to remain faithful to his teacher, Elijah Muhammad.

In subsequent years, as Farrakhan grew in stature, false accusations began to emerge that he had been involved in the assassination of Malcolm X. In an interview regarding the death of Malcolm X, Mike

Wallace of CBS News took words out of context in an attempt to align Farrakhan with the assassination. Spike Lee's movie *Malcolm X* (1992) portrays a skillful attempt to slow the momentum of the "Farrakhan phenomenon," as one actor portraying a newsperson asks, "Do you believe Farrakhan had something to do with it?"

Despite the barrage of negative media attention, Farrakhan was able to organize the Million Man March. On October 16, 1995, nearly two million Black men arrived in Washington, D.C., to hear a powerful lecture. Immediately following the March, Farrakhan embarked on a world tour of fifty-seven states, where he was greeted by world leaders and peoples of many nations. In Iran, he spoke to six or seven million people.

In several countries, his caravan was nearly overrun by people trying to touch him. (Final Call, ND). But back home in America, the news media described his friendship tour as time spent conversing with dictators. Thus, the ruling powers manipulated public opinion about Farrakhan, even going so far as getting some Black leaders to accuse him of squandering the good that could have come from the Million Man March.

For Farrakhan, the immediate years after the Million Man March were punctuated by declining health and close calls with death due to illness. In the more recent years, he appears to be physically and mentally rejuvenated holding four educational conferences that include powerful insights on education in the twenty-first century and beyond.

Additionally, on October 10, 2015, he led the twentieth anniversary of the Million Man March, which included a younger generation of youth who have witnessed the deaths of Black men at the hands of law enforcement. The march centered on the theme "Justice or Else" and is a movement that is all the more relevant with the protests following police killings in 2016. Farrakhan continues to be the most powerful Black leader in the twenty-first century.

The trials that he has experienced over a lifetime have brought him to new heights spiritually. In a rare interview with Alex Jones he began a dialogue that extends beyond the Black experience in America by offering compelling insight into the problems affecting all of humanity. (Final Call, 2016). To date he has not wavered in his mission to bring the whole of the human family into the knowledge of the time. The "Farrakhan phenomenon" is something that is beyond a personality; it is a deep embodiment of spiritual knowledge that I will attempt to dissect in the coming chapters.

Selected Works on Farrakhan and Education

Louis Farrakhan has been teaching for over fifty-five years. He began his ministerial work in 1955 when he became a member of the Nation of Islam and a student of Elijah Muhammad. During his early years in the Nation of Islam he worked closely with Malcolm X in New York's Mosque Number 7. After the death of Elijah Muhammad in 1975, he began to rebuild the Nation of Islam in 1978. Since that time he has delivered several speeches on education and leadership. The last eight years of his leadership have specifically focused on education and leadership. His addresses at historically black colleges and universities have further clarified his views on education. Out of the many lectures and writings on educational philosophy, the four that follow may be of particular interest to education scholars and students.

Education Is the Key

Published in 2006, this book by Minister Farrakhan delves into topics such as the goal of life, the education of women, knowledge beyond books, and mis-education. It is a good source for understanding philosophically Farrakhan's ideas about education. Particularly striking are the parallels with critical educational theory and multicultural education. For example in the section "Mis-Education and White Supremacy" he describes how those in power have shaped the educational agenda for Blacks. Speaking to this issue he writes, "If a man controls what goes in, he can control what comes out" (p. 20).

1. The Roots of Farrakhan's Educational Philosophy 9

Closing the Gap: Inner View of the Heart, Mind and Soul of the Honorable Minister Louis Farrakhan

In this book, Jabril Muhammad interviews Minister Farrakhan over the course of several years. This book is a jewel in describing his evolution as a student and leader in the Nation of Islam. It captures unique historical perspectives that detail how he became a member of the Nation of Islam and the suffering he endured during his early transition to Islam. Within the pages of the book the reader will find profound insights regarding education and leadership in the context of spirituality.

Education and The New Paradigm

This is a collection of twenty-seven lectures by Minister Farrakhan that speak specifically to education. For educational scholars, this is a treasure as it provides the context to understand Farrakhan's teachings comparatively to that of leading educational scholars.

The Education Challenge: A New Educational Paradigm for the 21st Century

This is a transcription of a lecture that Minister Farrakhan did in 2008 at an educational conference sponsored by the Muhammad University of Islam. The volume is a powerful critique of education in the United States. Drawing from statistics that cite educational decline Farrakhan declares that America has flatlined. In the context of critiquing contemporary education, he refers back to his teacher Elijah Muhammad to discuss the significance of knowledge saying, "Civilizations begin with knowledge and a civilization ends when the knowledge that originated that civilization ends" (p. 11).

Clearly, Farrakhan is concerned with the role of education in the society, particularly as it relates to those who have been historically underserved and oppressed. While the field of education over the last several years has begun to focus on issues of diversity, equity, and social justice at major national conferences, one of the most profound educators has been left out of the educational discourse. One might argue he is left out of the discourse because his critiques offer a true path for liberation. But we ignore his insights at our own peril.

Chapter 2:
The Prophetic Voice in Transforming Education

Louis Farrakhan has been involved in the educational uplift of those who have been on the margins of society for over fifty-five years. He has assumed the mission of his teacher, Elijah Muhammad, in leading the effort to bring Blacks in America into the knowledge of self. From 1955 to 1975 he was under the direct tutelage of Elijah Muhammad, being prepared to be sent into the world to effect human transformation first among the Blacks of America, then among Blacks throughout the world, and finally among the whole of humanity.

In February of 1975 Elijah Muhammad's death left Minister Farrakhan to carry on his legacy. Since that time, Farrakhan has been a voice crying in the wilderness, offering knowledge and direction to presidents, kings, political leaders, entertainers, gang leaders, scholars, and everyday people. Although his work has been viewed primarily within a political context, the key to understanding this historic figure may lie in examining his work from an education context.

When Elijah Muhammad met Wallace D. Fard in the 1930s, Fard had already invested time in studying various educational systems. Fard's conclusion about the American education system was that Blacks in America had been ill-served by its white supremacist ideology, and Muhammad considered that reforming education was one of his major callings. Farrakhan inherited this perspective and saw his mission as transforming education with the knowledge of self, which unlocks human potential and helps students to discover their divine essence and purpose for existence.

Most people view education as a system of strategies, methods, and lesson plans intended to prepare people for jobs. However, Farrakhan believes that the deeper significance of education is in a spiritual body of knowledge that includes the knowledge of God. And like Elijah Muhammad and W. D. Fard before him, he believes that American education not only denied students this spiritual knowledge but is also used as a tool of oppression.

Scholars have increasingly recognized that education is often designed to serve the best interest of those who rule the society (Asante, 1991; Darder, 2002; Freire, 2000; Giroux, 2015; McLaren, 2015; Watkins, 2001a, b; Woodson, 1999 [1933]). Chomsky (2000) calls this *mis-education* and contends that schools are "responsible for 'the indoctrination of the young.' The indoctrination is necessary because schools are, by and large, designed to support the interests of the dominant society, those people who have wealth and power" (p. 17).

The interests of the dominant society are served by preparing most children to be productive workers. Dominant society perpetuates the tactic of using education for sorting and selecting students for their roles in the society. Under the precepts of No Child Left Behind and Race to the Top, teachers are forced to teach test materials, not children. Public schools have become like fast food restaurants, throwing mostly useless knowledge—empty educational calories—at students.

The McDonaldization of education has resulted in deskilled teachers and administrators who are forced to essentially kill children's creativity (Giroux, 2015). Educators, particularly those serving non-White students, are given scripts to follow that any other person with reasonably good reading skills could follow. This has intellectually decapitated educators, leaving them disgruntled and uninspired.

In schools where poor or predominantly Black and Latino students make up the majority of the student population, the creative mind is put to death in the process of molding workers who will acquiesce to the status quo. Teachers and administrators openly decry the state of education but lack the knowledge to free themselves or their students.

As a result of schools' oppressive nature, some marginalized students revert to acts of violence against one another. Educators and parents are then tasked with resolving the social and educational dilemmas facing students: drug use, violence, apathy, the commercialization of schools, and the predatory culture of corporate America.

The hopelessness and reproduction of the status quo are major problems in our educational system. This is where Louis Farrakhan's ideas about education and society could offer a new way to address the social ills that confront society. Scholars of spirituality and education have chided that education must include the search for meaning and truth. Louis Farrakhan's educational ideas in areas like critical educational theory and human development could provide a paradigm shift in American education.

Historical Knowledge

One of the major challenges in preparing educators is the abundance of coursework focusing on technical skills such as lesson plans, assessment models, and the like. When queried about the purpose of education, most teachers have problems forming an answer. There is no consideration that the work of teaching is similar to a prophetic calling.

According to Elijah Muhammad, educators are the "torchlight of civilization," igniting fires in students' minds, giving them the energy and power to solve societal problems and thus advance civilization. Farrakhan (1993) explains, "Teachers are the stewards of the proper cultivation of people. Without teachers we have an undeveloped people" (p. 52).

To Farrakhan, educators are the catalyst for cultivating the divine essence in the human being. He writes, "So true education cultivates the person—mind, body, and spirit—by bringing us closer to fulfilling our purpose for being, which is to reflect Allah [God]" (p. 47). To fully understand the power of education in advancing civilization, educators need some historical knowledge.

What is particularly frightening about a majority of courses that prepare educators is that there is virtually no in-depth discussion about the history of American education from multicultural perspectives. Such a discussion would allow students to deconstruct how present conditions have been shaped by history. The study of marginalized groups is of little consequence, and too many schools of education attempt to make students believe that education is apolitical.

In education courses, some students would be shocked to read Asante's (1991) *Afrocentric Idea in Education*, Woodson's (1991) *Mis-Education of the Negro*, Sleeter's (2004) *White Racism*, King's (1991) *Dysconsious Racism*, Freire's (2000) *Pedagogy of the Oppressed*, McLaren's (2015) *Life in Schools*, Darder's (2002) *Reinventing Paulo Freire*, Nieto and Bode's (2012) *Affirming Diversity*, Howard's (2006) *We Can't Teach What We Don't Know*, Apple's (2004) *Official Knowledge*, Pinar's (2004) *What Is Curriculum Theory?*, or Pitre's (2015) *Educational Philosophy of Elijah Muhammad*. As a result, educators are left with little understanding of why schools operate the way they do.

Even worse, school leaders' training and preparation programs are distinctly technocratic in nature. For the most part, these programs produce educational managers, not leaders. Blount (1994) marks a contrast between the two positions: "Administrators are appointed by the persons to whom they must later account. Essentially, administrators tend to serve as functionaries whose roles are carefully defined, their hierarchical positions fixed" (p. 58).

Educational leaders thus become commissars for the state, pushing an official knowledge that serves the interest of the ruling elite (Apple, 2004; Chomsky, 2000) and acting somewhat as overseers of knowledge while being held accountable to school administrators through a system of surveillance-type measures. McKinney and Garrison (1994) note, "it is this bureaucratic record-keeping and technical devices of control [surveillance, observation, and comparative measures that are norm referenced] that make up the image of the modern administrator—the technocrat" (p. 78).

The No Child Left Behind Act of 2001, with its requirement that schools disaggregate data based on race, ethnicity, social class, and special needs, has created discourse around the disparities that exist between Black and White students. The teaching force, which is overwhelmingly comprised of White female teachers, is largely ignorant about the historical precedents that have shaped the educational reality of non-White students.

Often these teachers believe racism has been done away with; "That was in the past," they say. Even teachers or administrators with advanced degrees have had virtually no exposure to the great Black educators of history. People like Carter G. Woodson, Nanny Helen Burroughs, Elijah Muhammad, and others are noticeably absent in advanced textbooks and curricula. This monocultural education leaves educators ill-prepared to serve non-White students and transform schools.

We desperately need a new approach to educator training, one that includes the perspectives and wisdom of great Black educators. Critical Black pedagogy in education can be this approach. *Critical Black pedagogy in education* is an analysis of the White supremacist structure of education through an examination of the educational ideas of Black leaders and scholars who challenged it. Incorporating ideas grounded in critical Black pedagogy could help educators to learn how to overcome the oppressive school culture that dominates the school life of non-mainstream students.

Among the many thinkers whom critical Black pedagogy can introduce to teachers is Louis Farrakhan. In their book *A Pedagogy for Liberation*, critical educators Freire and Shor (1987) discuss the need to view social movements as an educational endeavor; this framing of education within social movements as liberation pedagogy uniquely fits the role of Louis Farrakhan. Yet educational scholars have not examined the knowledge he disclosed to ignite passion in Black men to atone for wrongs done to themselves and others. In the next section, we examine what may be gleaned from one of Farrakhan's most important projects, the Million Man March, regarding the possibilities for transforming schools.

A Million Black Men as Teachers

In the public school environment, which is comprised of a predominantly homogenous teaching force, Black students—especially Black males—are often feared by teachers, regardless of their age. One principal disclosed that she had to send home a four-year-old Black male student because of a conflict with a White pre-K teacher, who was terrified of the little boy (Personal Communication, 2009). Just as teachers are often fearful of Black children, teachers and administrators were fearful of Native American children, who were once sent to boarding schools where the motto was kill the Indian, save the man.

In both cases, the teachers were not equipped to create environments that acknowledged the students' humanity, much less empower the students to overcome the problems of their everyday lives and thrive. Still today, the cultural incongruity between White teachers and Black students is so apparent that Black children are alienated in school, and thus alienated from themselves.

When Louis Farrakhan called for one million men to assemble and march on the National Mall in Washington, D.C., no one examined this prolific gathering as an educational endeavor that could transform the condition of life for oppressed and marginalized peoples. This was not simply accomplished by getting on a microphone; it was Farrakhan's tremendous knowledge that moved Black Men to hearken to his message. The teachings that undergirded the Million Man March, if properly understood and applied, could also be used to increase the Black male presence in schools.

Imagine the potential impact of thousands of Black male teachers equipped with the proper knowledge and the spirit of the Million Man March in schools across America. What is so compelling about this possibility is that the majority of the men who attended the Million Man March were committed to changing their communities; this same energy and spirit could be transferred to schools in America and abroad.

The day before the Men's Only Meeting (one of Minister Farrakhan's speaking tours prior to the Million Man March) in New Orleans, there was a basketball game in one of the housing projects.

2. The Prophetic Voice in Transforming Education 17

During the game, a scuffle broke out and escalated to the point of one participant going to his car to get a weapon. Fortunately, no one was hurt, but what was shocking was that one of the individuals involved in the scuffle was at the Men's Only Meeting the next day!

He was just one of the countless men from diverse backgrounds who packed the University of New Orleans Lakefront Arena that day to hear knowledge emanating from Farrakhan. Regardless of background, he taught these men—or, students—profound truths that captivated their attention. Reflecting on this experience, there are possibilities for gleaning from this historic moment; opportunities to create an educational movement that could liberate the divine essence in human beings.

To date, there is no university that can boast a teacher education population that comprises of thousands of Black men. To effectively educate thousands of Black men to become teachers would require a different organizational structure than what is currently in place. Additionally, the essential elements that undergird Farrakhan's spiritual messages could be used to develop an educational curriculum for educators. This would not be difficult to do, as there are several colleges of education and universities across America with conceptual frameworks that align with the Nation of Islam's teachings. While this utopian vision may seem far-fetched in the current world, it holds great possibility for the new world on the horizon.

Understanding the organizational and educational structure that gave rise to the Million Man March could lead to an increase in Black men becoming educators. The call to be an educator is beyond the current simplistic version of technocratic teaching; it is a prophetic call to be, as Elijah Muhammad declared it, "saviors." At the 2011 Saviors Day convention, Minister Farrakhan (2011) delivered a message entitled "God Will Send Saviors" that highlighted the need for saviors, highlighting "that one is making many saviors to send them, to save a people distressed and oppressed" (p. 3). These saviors would perhaps be great teachers "who have a genuine love for people and a desire to bring the best out of our children" (Farrakhan, 1993, p. 53).

It may seem strange to approach education from such a spiritual standpoint, to cite the need to awaken "divine essence," and for teachers to be "saviors." But without a spiritual component, one that addresses lifting students up to their greatest human potential, then school just becomes vocational training and serves to perpetuate current inequities rather than fix them. The next section clarifies the spiritual aspect of Farrakhan's educational thinking.

Spirituality and Education

In the field of education, there is a body of knowledge that particularly examines education and spirituality. Educational scholars in this area contend that the spiritual components of education have been sidelined and that education can be transformed by inculcating the spiritual into the schooling experience. For example, Pinar et al. (2008) highlight these connections in *Understanding Curriculum*. It is because of the importance of reintroducing the spiritual component into education that Farrakhan's teachings should be examined.

Farrakhan expounded on the philosophy of Elijah Muhammad regarding education. During an interview granted to the National Education Television, Muhammad (1965) described his mission this way: "My mission is to bring life to the dead. What I teach brings them out of death and into life" (p. 306). In referring to raising the dead, Muhammad is specifically referring to the *mental* death of Black people, who in Freire's (2000) description of the oppressed, had been made beings for others.

Muhammad argues, "All the history of Islam never reveals anything that any man had ever been able to come back from a physical death. But there is a chance for mental death because the lost found was once dead mentally and many of them revived from it" (Muhammad, 1993, p. 18). Reversing the mental death of Black people would mean awakening their creative minds and empowering them to build a world never before witnessed.

In Muhammad's *Message to the Blackman in America* (1965), he speaks again of using education to unleash the best within us in order to advance civilization: "The duty of the civilized man is to teach civilization to the uncivilized—the arts and sciences of civilized people and countries of advanced civilization ... A well-educated, cultured, and courteous people make a beautiful society when it is spiritual. Good manners come from the civilized man who does not fail to perform his duty" (p. 44). The failure of American education in this regard is obvious. Violence permeates schools as well as the larger society, suggesting that schools have not really educated the human being.

Louis Farrakhan echoed all of these principles in his own writings. He posited, "True and proper education starts with the knowledge of God. And yet God is taken out of schools ... The knowledge of God is infinite. I would argue that leaving God out of our schools limits our education and confines the scope of what we are equipped to do and achieve" (p. 48).

Some might argue that Farrakhan's perspective mirrors that of conservative educators. Regarding the conservative tradition, Spring (2011) writes, "By linking American exceptionalism to Christianity, religious-oriented conservatives believe that any attack on the role of religion in government is an attack on the very foundations of American life" (p. 129). However, contrary to the message of conservatives who may hold a Euro-centered, White supremacist perspective of God, Farrakhan is speaking to awakening the divine essence in every human being.

Awakening the divine essence means unlocking each student's potential and also deconstructing the hidden curriculum of White supremacy. Francis Wesling (1991) alludes to the way conservative views of God have morphed into an ideology of White supremacy:

> Couple this image and concept of God as a white man with the white supremacy system's formal definition of God as the supreme or ultimate reality; the Being perfect in power, wisdom and whom men worship as creator and ruler of the universe. Then of absolute necessity, the logic circuits of the

human brain computer have to print out the white man is the supreme or ultimate reality; the white man is the Being, perfect in power, wisdom and goodness whom all men should worship as creator and ruler of the universe. (p. 168)

Farrakhan's work has sought to destroy the White supremacist and Black inferiority complexes that have caused societal decay. Speaking to the problem of education and why there is a need to move beyond the superficial, he explains, "The problem in today's education is that the root motivation is the acquisition of wealth and material things rather than the cultivation of the human spirit" (p. 47).

Educators who see their roles as more than a job for material gain would more than likely agree with Farrakhan's (1993) note on the second purpose of education, which is "after self-cultivation … to teach us how to give proper service to self, family, community, nation, and then to the world" (p. 47). He encourages a new type of education predicated on the principles of freedom, justice, and equality:

If America does not wake up and recognize the consequences of perpetuating the current system of education, then the country's fate is sealed. If America is unwilling to destroy the old system of education in order to create a new system of education, then America's status as a world power will quickly fade away in a generation or so. (p. 46)

Farrakhan joins other educational thinkers in fulfilling a prophetic role in society. Purpel and McLaurin (2004) write, "Prophets were passionate social critics who applied sacred criteria to human conduct and, when they found violations of these criteria they cried out in anguish and outrage" (p. 89).

In the field of education, there are many voices that have cried out for a new and better educational system based on freedom, justice, and equality (Banks, 2014; Darder, 2002; Nieto and Bode, 2012; Gollnick and Chinn, 2017; Ladson-Billings, 2009a; McLaren, 2015; Howard, 2006; Pitre, 2011; Starratt, 2004; Sleeter and Grant, 2009).

2. The Prophetic Voice in Transforming Education

Farrakhan is clearly part of this tradition of social criticism and passionate "anguish and outrage." As he wrote, Blacks in America were

> mis-educated and taught against ourselves, so our education was not real because it was not based on complete truth. It was based on the psychology of White supremacy and reinforced in the minds of Black people that we must accept our subhuman posture and position, and remember White people are born to rule and we must never rise to challenge that rule. (Farrakhan, 2006, p. 21)

Farrakhan does, in fact, apply "sacred criteria" to human conduct. He speaks, for example, of reading: "White people never really learned to read, for if they had learned to read the universe, they would have understood, as Thomas Jefferson said, 'I tremble for my country when I reflect that God is just and that his justice cannot sleep forever'" (p. 21). What good is it to know how to read words and you cannot "read" the injustice written all over our world and thus work to rectify it?

It is the prophetic nature of Farrakhan's social criticism that has caused him to be cast him as a "prophet of rage" by the media (Magida, 1996). Purpel and McLaughlin (2004) term this the *prophetic dilemma* and argue that prophets of old "were often consulted by the priests and kings and sometimes, nevertheless, imprisoned for their views and agitations" (p. 113).

Farrakhan's prophetic utterances remind America and the world that justice cannot sleep forever, and his calls for change are deeply unsettling to those who are invested in the status quo. Farrakhan is problematic because he has the ability to articulate in an uncompromising way the gross inequalities existing in society. He has been viewed as the voice of millions of Black people all over the world; however, his work should be viewed as universal, extending beyond Blacks in America to all of humanity. A spiritual education is intended to lift all people to their greatest potential.

Farrakhan and Education

Howard (2006) speaks to the necessity of self-reflection for those in the dominant group: "One of the dilemmas of White dominance is that we are often blind to the negative impact that our imagined goodness and narrow sense of normalcy have on others who do not share the demographic advantages that have favored our group" (p. 120). In Howard's view, White educators and people in general must always be engaged in a process of becoming. This is partly in the cause of justice for others but also a matter of developing their own divine essence rather than serving gods of greed and power.

When it was reported in 2007 that Farrakhan was extremely ill and near death, he emerged at the February Savior's Day event to give what some thought might be his last speech. He declared that, while being a voice for suffering Black people, he could not turn a blind eye to the suffering of the *whole* of humanity. He noted that people of many different races, ethnicities, social classes, and religious perspectives had offered prayers for his healing. As a result, his grave illness had shown him the need to emphasize that his mission is universal in scope. Speaking to both the spiritual and universal components of education, he writes:

> Take knowledge and let it give you a heart for the suffering people who are your own and the suffering people of the world … Put on the whole armor of God and stand against the wiles of the wicked, that a better world may come into existence. Take the key of the knowledge from the Messiah and close the door on an old world that has given us all so much pain, and open the door with that key to a better world. In that world, we will live as Black, Brown, Red, Yellow and White and there will no longer be a need to mention color again. In that world you will never be judged by the color of your skin, but by your deeds and intentions. (Farrakhan, 2006, p. 29)

There is a universal aspect of Louis Farrakhan's work that is not always clearly visible but that is one of the keys to his leadership, not

2. The Prophetic Voice in Transforming Education

only for Blacks in America but for the millions of voiceless and oppressed peoples throughout the earth. It is incumbent upon all of us to gain knowledge of ourselves through an education that is spiritual in nature, and not just vocational.

Chapter 3:
Determining the Purpose of Education

One of the major questions confronting educators, students, and the general public is, "What is the purpose of education?" Educational philosophers have proposed a variety of theories about what education should entail. Daily the airwaves and newspapers tout the great need for a better educational system. Politicians in every state contend that education is crucial to the survival of their states and the nation.

But before education can be fixed, we must determine what its purpose is. To get on the "right track," we need to know where we are intending the voyage to take us. To do that, this chapter examines three major philosophies of education and compares them with the educational philosophy of Louis Farrakhan. Each of them proposes a different answer to that most basic question: What is the purpose of education?

The Roots of Public Education

As public education expanded throughout the United States, Gatto (2002) notes, wealthy philanthropists like the Rockefellers, DuPonts, Morgans, and Carnegies, among others, spent considerable money developing it in ways that coincided with their own philosophies of education. The Rockefellers, for example, committed "millions upon millions of dollars ... to Negro Education, as this family concentrated on becoming financiers, ideologists, and architects of Black Education" (Watkins, 2001a, p. 118).

As these early contributors demonstrate, education has always been an essential platform piece for those who rule society, compelling them to spend considerable amounts of money on the development of the world's educational systems to ensure that people are educated to fit their ideas about what society should look like. These early philanthropists created foundations that had greater influence on education than even the government.

Watkins (2001a) writes, "Elected by no one, these agencies wielded government-like power. Accountable to only themselves, they were private entities making sweeping educational and public policy. Because they could totally finance and administer projects, their actions had the effect of law" (p. 20). These philanthropists were actually using their wealth for the purpose of social engineering; and the resulting educational system, according to Spivey (2007), was a new form of slavery for Blacks.

These power structures are still intact, as foundations and think tanks funded by those with significant wealth continue to influence education. In his book *The Politics of American Education*, Joel Spring (2011) tackles the relationship between wealth and educational reform

> Besides supporting charter schools and national designs for charter schools, the Gates Foundation and President Obama's administration shared an interest in creating a national school data bank to measure schools, teachers, principals, and teacher training institutions ... For the cynical and conspiratorially minded, Bill Gates and his Foundation's emphasis on data systems might be linked to his continued ownership of Microsoft shares and potential sale of software geared to national-common standards. (pp. 24–25)

The push for data banks coincides with the preparation programs for educational leaders that emphasize the need to base all decisions on data. Additionally, the push for data aligns with the No Child

Left Behind Act of 2001 and Race to the Top, which focus on test scores as measurement data. Sadly, the emphasis on data has caused teachers to become test administrators rather than educators. Nearly every teacher you talk to laments the new push to "teach to the test" rather than teaching what children need and helping them to grow as full human beings. The push for data has created inauthentic learning: It has forced educators to ignore the true purpose of education while allowing those in power to use test scores to sort students without the public ever asking who decides what will be tested.

And considering the alarming frequency with which Black and Latino students are being labeled as deficient because of their test scores, it appears that a mind game is being played in order to relegate the masses of students in public schools to a certain form of life. Spring (2011) maintains that the philosophy driving these new policies is based on human capitalist economics:

> Today, the dominant educational ideology is human capital economics, which defines the primary goal of education as economic growth, in contrast to other ideologies that might emphasize the passing on of culture or the education of students for social justice. Human capital economics contains a vision of school as a business preparing workers for businesses. (p. 6)

What becomes clear is that students are seen as a labor supply and not necessarily as authentic human beings with a divine essence that must be cultivated. Because education is the key to creating a society, it cannot be left to chance; thus, those with great financial power take great pains to develop schools that serve their interests.

To effectively dismantle the current practice of education that Freire (2000) describes as domesticating and dehumanizing, there is a need to have some knowledge of the different philosophical views about education. This knowledge can help educators deconstruct the current practice of education. This chapter examines three major philosophical canons that have shaped contemporary ideas about the purpose of education. Judging by how these philosophers' canonical contributions—in particular the concepts of idealism, realism, pragmatism, and behaviorism—have been revered in the field of education, it could be concluded that to this point, dead White men continue to rule the educational discourse.

Philosophical Canons

Idealism

One of the earliest schools of Western philosophy is idealism, a philosophy contending that ideas constitute the only true reality. It harkens back to Socrates, who believed that education should help one to know the self. He proffered that great ideas lay dormant inside the individual and required certain stimuli to bring these ideas to the forefront of consciousness.

He used a method of questioning (the Socratic method) designed to induce students to recall or bring forth ideas; idealists argue that this method is representative of the search for truth. This raises the question, What is truth? Ozmon and Craver (2008) write that idealists like Socrates and later Augustine believed that truth was God: "According to Augustine, the search for truth is a search for God, and a true education leads one to God. Because God is pure idea, God can be reached only through contemplation of ideas; therefore, a true education is concerned with ideas rather than matter" (p. 21).

The idea of God has been of central concern to philosophers of all canons but is clearly one of the main contentions of idealists who believe in mind over matter. This is evident in the link between idealist thought and scriptural writings (e.g., Descartes' "I think therefore I am" coincides with the biblical text "For as a man thinketh in his heart so is he"). Idealists like Horne believed "education should encourage the 'will to perfection' for the student and is an activity whereby one shapes oneself into the likeness of God—a task that requires eternal

3. Determining the Purpose of Education

life for its fulfillment" (Ozmon and Craver, 2008, p. 23). Clearly, idealists were concerned with questions about God.

The Nation of Islam has this in common with idealism: It begins its education program by asking, "Who is God?" But contrary to idealists who base their philosophy on ideas in search of God as truth, Elijah Muhammad declared that the term *god* means one superior in knowledge, wisdom, and understanding (Hakim, 1997b). For Farrakhan, education must begin by teaching children that they are gods—that they have within them a divine essence that, once awoken, can allow them to achieve great things. In part, this coincides with Freire's (2000) advocacy of students' viewing themselves as actors in the world rather than passive receptacles waiting to be filled. For Farrakhan (1993), the purpose of education is divine:

> Let's deal with what education is supposed to be as opposed to what it is in America. One of the things that separates man from beast is knowledge. Knowledge feeds the development of human beings so that the person can grow and evolve into Divine and become one with the Creator. It's not one's maleness or femaleness, being Black or being White; rather it is our growth and reflection of knowledge that distinguishes us from lower forms of life. (p. 47)

The knowledge that serves as the springboard to bring the individual into oneness with the Creator is the same knowledge that propels the student to uncover their own divine essence. Elijah Muhammad called this the knowledge of self; twentieth-century philosopher and idealist J. Donald Butler called it self-realization:

> Accordingly, he [Butler] finds that the self is the prime reality of individual experience; that ultimate reality can be conceived of as a self; and that it might be one self, a community of selves, or a Universal Self; hence, education

becomes primarily concerned with self realization. (Ozmon and Craver, 2008, p. 22)

Similarly, Farrakhan believes that true education helps fulfill the individual's purpose for existence so that they can be of service to "self, family, community, nation and then to the world" (p. 47).

Clearly, there are similarities between Butler's and Farrakhan's assertions; in fact, many ideas of these early western philosophers can be traced back to the African continent. In the book *Stolen Legacy*, which was banned from colleges and universities up until 1954, George James (2001) contends that several of the great western philosophers stole knowledge from the "ancient mystery schools of Egypt," which illuminated knowledge starkly similar to the teachings of Elijah Muhammad.

James (2001) writes that one key goal of education espoused by the ancient mystery schools of Egypt "was to make a man godlike by the purificatory agencies of education and virtue" (p. 72). Elijah Muhammad disclosed that the ultimate aim of education is to make gods: "Every one of you according to what God has taught me will be Gods ... We have power if restored to what we originally were, but we have been robbed of the knowledge of self" (Hakim 1997b, p. 272). Farrakhan (1983) elaborated: "The Honorable Elijah Muhammad has taught us that the purpose for knowledge is to feed the development of the human being until that human grows into divine and becomes a true manifestation of the characteristics of God" (p. 4).

The philosophical cornerstone of proper education has consistently been formed by ideas about God; thus, the question of God becomes very problematic for educators who are told that they must separate church from state in the classroom. Interestingly, Sagini (1996) observes that in the ancient universities, theology was considered the Queen of the Sciences. It was the quest to know God that gave birth to great discoveries in science and played a role in the establishment of laws in all of the disciplines.

Farrakhan opposes the modern concept of schooling that has eliminated God from school, believing that, "True and proper education starts with the knowledge of God. And yet God is taken out of the schools ... The knowledge of God is infinite. I would argue that leaving God out of our schools limits our education and confines our scope of what we are equipped to do and achieve" (Farrakhan 1993, p. 48).

Realism

Realists contend that education should extend beyond the study of ideas to include the study of matter. Aristotle, a student of Plato, believed that although ideas were important, the study of matter could provide a better understanding of ideas—that in fact, ideas should come from our study of matter. On the question of God, the realist argument can be found in Aristotle's reasoning that "ideas such as the idea of God or the idea of a tree cannot exist without matter, but no matter can exist without form" (Ozmon and Craver 2008, p. 40). Realists argue that ultimately, matter is progressing toward some end predetermined by the Unmoved Mover, or the Ultimate Reality. What is striking is that the realist perspective is also grounded in ideas presented in the ancient mystery schools as well as the teachings of Elijah Muhammad.

One early relative of realism was the pre-Socratic thinkers who discussed at length what the universe was made of. They conceptualized that the universe was composed of small particles that combined to make our material world, essentially discovering the atom. According to James (2001), "The atom is described as full or solid, invisible, indestructible, uncreated, and capable of self-motion. The atoms differ in shape, order, position, quantity, and weight" (p. 65).

Elijah Muhammad also focused on the atom as the building block of material life. He taught that the origin of life began when the first atom sparkled in the darkness. This atom began to move, which was the beginning of time:

> The beginning of time was made by the beginning of God. We had no beginning before; there was no motion making time until after he made himself. He made motion, and we've been reading time ever since … In the making of God himself, he could not have had will until he had brains capable of thinking. He was self-created from an Atom of life. (Hakim, 1997b, pp. 152, 183–184)

The atom described by Elijah Muhammad is moving and becomes the unmoved mover, the ultimate reality. Farrakhan provides an explanation from the teachings of Elijah Muhammad that speaks on the same topic to capture the essence of education:

> There's matter in the darkness. It is considered nothing because it has neither form nor function, but it's matter. So, now he's [God's] forming. As he forms himself, he studies himself. Then he makes a reality that corresponds with himself. Well, later he said let there be light. There was already light in him. The Honorable Elijah Muhammad says, "He was a light of himself." So what he did was bring out of himself a reality and put it in a beautiful form and gave it purpose to manifest who he is. (Muhammad, 2006, p. 263)

This captures the duality that realists and idealists were grappling with. Opposed to setting up distinct philosophical canons, Farrakhan discloses the unity of ideas and matter. Education, then, should help us define and bring into existence a reality that corresponds with our purpose for existence.

Pragmatism

Pragmatist educational philosophers believe that education should have some practical purpose and should be connected to students' experiences. In this sense the curriculum should primarily serve the purpose of helping students become acquainted with the world in relation to their interaction with it.

John Dewey, a leading educational philosopher, was considered by some to be a pragmatist and a humanist; however, like idealist and realist philosophers, Dewey seems to have grappled with issues of theology, as evidenced by his belief that children should be educated in a way that allows them to discover their powers. This is similar to the idea that children should be helped by education to discover their divine essence.

In *My Pedagogic Creed*, Dewey (1897) writes that education has two inseparable foundations: psychological and sociological. The first deals with developing the child's mental powers, while the second is concerned with preparing the student for life in a social world. Dewey contends, "In order to know what a power really is we must know what its end, use, or function is, and this we cannot know save we conceive of the individual as active in social relationships" (p. 5).

Pragmatism is concerned with the practice of education and the question, What is its end? This coincides with the teachings of Elijah Muhammad and can be seen in Farrakhan's work as his national representative. Sections of the *Supreme Wisdom* study book (a book for students in the Nation of Islam) that relate to pragmatism deal with spookism and the use of mathematics in connection with Islam. The book poses this question to students in the Nation of Islam about waiting for a spook God to produce a world: "Will you sit at home and wait for that mystery God to bring you food?" (Muhammad, 1993, p. 18).

Students are admonished that there is no spook God; whatever they have the mental capacity to conceive in their minds, they have the ultimate responsibility for making a reality. This was the basis of Elijah Muhammad's "do for self" program, designed to create the mindset that his students had the power to change their reality and must thus use their knowledge for the practical purpose of building a nation and a world.

In *Education Is the Key* (2006), Farrakhan argues that knowledge is power that must be put to some practical use. Supreme Wisdom extends this to the way of life called Islam. The practice or way of Islam is not simply reading the Quran, praying, or practicing the five pillars of Islamic faith; it is a mathematical process that gives its adherents knowledge to live the highest form of life.

The Supreme Wisdom declares that mathematics is Islam and Islam is mathematics; "then you must learn to use it and secure some benefit while you are living, that is luxury, money, good homes, friendship in all walks of life" (Muhammad, 1993, p. 6). This coincides with the Nation of Islam's teaching that heaven is not meant to be passively awaited but produced on Earth.

While many would argue that heaven is in outer space, the Nation of Islam's belief is rooted in a prayer found in scripture, oft referred to as the Lord's Prayer: "Our Father which art in heaven, hallowed be thy name. Thy kingdom come, thy will be done in earth as it is in heaven" (Matthew 6:9–10, King James Version).

In this prayer, the kingdom of God on earth must be produced by real people who should not wait to die before accessing heaven. Elijah Muhammad avows that heaven is a place that people create, not some special place they must go. This kind of teaching could potentially create a social, political, and economic revolution among Blacks who had been taught through the western construction of Christianity that their suffering on Earth at the hands of their slave masters would result in passage to heaven after their deaths. The Nation of Islam vehemently opposed such teaching, declaring that this type of Christianity was a slave-making religion that benefited the rulers of the society (Muhammad,1965). Instead the Nation of Islam advocated a pragmatist approach, one in which humans act to change the world.

Moral and Spiritual Crisis in Education

Elijah Muhammad and Louis Farrakhan contend that "education banishes savagery." The daily news accounts of murder, theft, and other crimes have reached a climactic point. In fact, it has been argued that this type of savagery has never before been experienced in the modern or postmodern world.

Scholars in the field of education have argued that education is a matter of moral and spiritual concern. Purpel and McLaurin (2004) contend that education must extend beyond the technical: "Our cultural crisis is a crisis in meaning, and this crisis can therefore be seen basically as moral and religious; we need to see this crisis in education as not primarily problems of technique, organization, and funding but as a reflection of the crisis of meaning" (p. 41).

Starratt (2004) believes one of the major problems with schools is their inability to instill a sense of caring in students. He argues that what happens in schools is not authentic learning but fake learning, which in turn produces fake people:

> I say this out of conviction that the learning achieved by students is generally superficial and largely decontextualized from student experience and the life of the community. In other words, it is inauthentic learning, superficial learning, fake learning, make believe learning, rather than something that intrinsically adds value to students' lives and prepares them for responsible adulthood ... Basically, schools and teachers are teaching youngsters to master the art of inauthentic learning, which amounts to schools teaching youngsters to be inauthentic. (pp. 2–3)

Farrakhan (2006) similarly argues that the problem of education is spiritual in nature, related to the development of character, which is vitally important and the loftiest of goals:

> In the language of religion, the loftiest goal for which men and women should strive is the development of their character; their character should reflect the Divine Supreme Being. This is the greatest of goals, not to have a Ph.D. degree. Even though you are so blessed if you have one, to have a degree of knowledge and not the high degree of character means that your degree serves vain purposes. To be knowledgeable and wicked makes us devils in human form. To be

knowledgeable and righteous makes us men and women of distinction. (pp. 6–7)

Today, schools purposely shy away from the moral and spiritual development of students because this would instill values that are inconsistent with those of the rulers of society. The actual goal of some schools is to diminish students' natural tendency to seek knowledge, particularly spiritual knowledge that would awaken their god consciousness.

Farrakhan points out that during the first year of life, a baby learns more than at any other point in life—and without the presence of an actual teacher. What we can observe from these babies is the quest for knowledge. They are constantly digging, experimenting, trying to discover and understand the world they have recently entered. Once in school, however, this creative exploratory tendency is put to sleep under the guise of gaining knowledge. The end result is that students are turned off to learning, particularly students in schools with a predominantly non-mainstream student population.

Some might argue that the prophets had a body of knowledge designed to transform the individual and the society. Farrakhan (2009) explains, "All the prophets and messengers of God and the sages that are recorded in history brought with them knowledge, or a light. A torchlight is a guiding principle, so education must guide the civilization. And inherent in that education is the idea that fuels that civilization" (p.11).

Embedded in the prophets' messages was knowledge that the people did not possess; however, this knowledge produced ideas that advanced the civilizations where they taught. Even today, those who await the return of Christ expect his coming because he brings knowledge that will change their lived reality, giving them "life more abundantly" (John 10:10, King James Version). Farrakhan (2006) posits,

> You are really looking for the solution to the problem of education, but the solution is not in the system that nurtured you—it's in a man … The Honorable Elijah Muhammad said

life is the embodiment of three great principles: Freedom, Justice, and Equality. When a man says, "I am the bread of life. If you eat my flesh, you will never hunger. And if you believe, you will never thirst," that is a man bringing with him the knowledge to give freedom, justice, and equality to every living being on our planet. (p. 20)

Essential to creating a new world is a body of knowledge that supersedes what is currently being disseminated in schools all over the world. Under the current system it is very difficult for educators and students to fulfill the true purpose of education, which is ultimately about unlocking students' creative minds to help them discover their divine essence or life purpose. Starratt (2004) brilliantly observes that once in school, students are bombarded with

> an academic body of knowledge "out there somewhere" that someone—this ambiguous thing called the state or the future job market or the adult world—requires them to study and figure out well enough to pass quizzes and tests, knowledge that is almost entirely removed from the realities they experience outside school. (p. 2)

Thus students in this type of educational system start to hate both school and the natural acquisition of more knowledge, which eventually results in bestiality from the lack of knowledge of self. Farrakhan (2009) addressed it thus:

> So when we look at the problems of the society, and the problems of education, it is demonstrative of the fact that this education and the idea that undergirds it has reached its end. And as the torchlight of this civilization is going out, that fact is reflected in the culture, the degeneracy of the culture, the degeneracy of the art form. It is reflected in the immorality, the debauchery, the lust for pleasure through drugs and sex. (p. 14)

He argues that some of the blame for the lack of a moral and spiritual consciousness in human beings falls on those who control education, described as bestial creatures with a kindergarten mentality:

> Now look, the beast is in control of a human being who has a kindergarten mentality. Now when you're in kindergarten—this word "Kinder" comes from a German word "das kind," which means "the children," and "Garten" means garden, and a garden is a fertile, delightful spot where you plant seeds. Now if all of us are like children in a garden, and a beast is planting seeds in our brains, then when you grow up to be what you call mature, how do you act? (Eure and Jerome 1989, p. 237)

Thus, it becomes important for educators to understand the history and politics of education. This knowledge would result in what the Nation of Islam calls *root knowledge*, or knowledge that uncovers how the present has been shaped by the past. When provided with these deeper historical understandings, educators and students could begin to deconstruct the current practice of education, moving them to work toward bringing forth a new kind of educational system—one that would capture the true purpose of education.

Chapter 4:
Farrakhan and the Human Development Approach to Education

Human development is a major area of study for students entering the education profession. However, in the study of human development there is very little discourse that mentions the connection between spirituality and human development. In this regard, the teachings of Louis Farrakhan provide an opportunity to extend the discussion to a new realm that connects spirituality with human development. This chapter covers three major connecting ideas about human development: Newman and Newman's work on human development, the nature/nurture debate, and the role of creativity in education and development.

Newman and Newman's Human Development

Newman and Newman (2009) use a theoretical approach to understanding human development called the psychosocial theory, which espouses that there are three main areas that should be examined when studying human development: biological, psychological, and social. They contend that what happens in any of these areas affects the process of human development.

For example, if a child suffers from malnutrition, this will have an impact on the child's psychological and social development. They note, "Psychosocial theory presents human development as a product of ongoing interaction between the individual (psycho) biological and psychological needs and abilities on the one hand and the societal (social) expectations and demands on the other hand" (p. 20).

In discussing the psychological, which forms the basis for understanding human development, the psyche is referred to as the soul. While the soul is key in the spiritual realm, some have argued that psychiatrists who work with human development have been more concerned with the animalistic side of the human being. What has developed as a result of focusing on this animalistic side is an educational center that is more concerned with training or conditioning than educating people. Gatto (2002) writes, "Schools are intended to produce, through the application of formulas, formulaic human beings whose behavior can be predicted and controlled" (p. 23).

One of the basic concepts presented by Newman and Newman (2009) is the theory of psychosocial evolution proposed by Julian Huxley (cited in Newman and Newman, 2009), which is concerned with understanding the range of abilities that allows human beings to gather information from the past and transfer this knowledge to their descendants. For Newman and Newman (2009), the theory of psychosocial evolution "is the study of the evolutionary origins of mental structures, emotions, and social behavior ... evolutionary psychology draws on the principles of evolution to understand the human mind" (p. 45).

Both the psychosocial and psychoevolution theories have implications that can be found in the Nation of Islam's teachings. In particular, the theory of psychoevolution, with its concern about the range of human abilities as it relates to gathering information about one's past in order to transmit this knowledge to future generations, has linkages to the Nation of Islam's teachings about the knowledge of self.

Elijah Muhammad (1965) argued that the knowledge of self was missing from the education of Black people. According to his teachings, this knowledge would open a range of human abilities that had thus far been asleep in the Black man and woman of America. In gaining the knowledge of self, Black people would gain knowledge of their past, understand their contemporary world, and be empowered to usher in a new world.

The Nation of Islam's problem book highlights this point: "The Laborers must speak and use grammatical pronunciation of words and syllables in past, present, future, and perfect tense" (Muhammad, 1993, p. 3). Speaking the language correctly means being able to understand how the past impacts the present and how things can be perfected in the future. Regarding the knowledge of self and the similarities with psychosocial evolution, Elijah Muhammad (1965) writes:

> I am for the acquiring of knowledge or the accumulating of knowledge as we now call it, education. First, my people must be taught the knowledge of self. Then and only then will they be able to understand others and that which surrounds them. Anyone who does not have a knowledge of self is considered a victim of either amnesia or unconsciousness and is not very competent. (p. 39)

Thus, Blacks in America must be reeducated, and at the root of that education is the knowledge of self, God, and the times. These areas of knowledge form the basis of a curriculum that will deliver Blacks in America from the mental death that has occurred as a result of the slavery experience.

A major part of the process of enslavement was the stripping of knowledge that would empower Blacks in America to access their history. Farrakhan alludes to the power of history and the psychoevolutionary struggle of Blacks:

> History shows us the realm of human possibility. If you don't know what you did, then you don't know what you can do, so if you're robbed of that kind of information, then what everyone else does becomes your and my standard, and their standard may be far beneath what our standard should be, but you will never know that until you get acquainted with your own history. (Eure and Jerome, 1989, p. 48)

Being stripped of their history and denied a true and proper knowledge of themselves has created behaviors for Black people that are not natural to the "Blackman." The natural behaviors of Black people, according to Farrakhan, are "good and right" (Farrakhan, 1992, p. 31). Naim Akbar (1998) also reflects on the necessity of having knowledge of one's history. Similar to ideas found in the psychoevolution theory he writes:

> We know now that people who have survived exposure to certain diseases are able to transmit immunity to those diseases through their genes, the mother's blood while in the womb, or from the mother's milk while being breast-fed ... this serves the analogy for another of the functions of education. In addition to bringing forth of identity and transmitting the legacy of competence, education must also transmit many of the acquire immunities that have been learned by earlier generations and their exposure to a variety of intellectual and social diseases. (p. 9)

One of the main problems with the education of Blacks in America is that they do not control the system. As result, Black students in too many schools are deprived of a true and proper education. In years past, Blacks were deprived of knowledge through force and in several cases were severely punished for the pursuit of knowledge. Joel Spring (2010) writes, "Literacy was a punishable crime for enslaved Africans in the South. However, by the outbreak of the Civil War in 1860, it is estimated that 5 percent of slaves had learned how to read, sometimes at the risk of life or limb" (p. 53).

Today, schools employ a similar strategy, which forces Black students to engage a curriculum purposely constructed to create an alien identity that Akbar (1998) describes as *mis-education*: "When people are taught they are somebody who they are not, then this forms the basis of being mis-educated" (p. 5). Elijah Muhammad (1965) spoke to this in relation to the knowledge of self:

> There is much misunderstanding among us because of our inferior knowledge of self. We have been to the schools where they do not teach us the knowledge of self. We have been to the schools of our slave-master children. We have been to their schools and gone as far as they have allowed us to go. That was not far enough for us to learn the knowledge of self. The lack of knowledge of self is one of our main handicaps. It blocks us throughout the world. (p. 34)

The knowledge of self empowers one to seek knowledge and acts as the stimulus for behavior. One of the major discussions concerning teachers is the behavior of students, particularly Black males—who have higher suspension and expulsion rates than their White peers. Problem student behavior brings up another major concern, particularly for new teachers: anxiety about classroom management. To effectively curtail many of the problems that both teachers and students experience in schools, it is essential that teachers be prepared to design pedagogy that supports students acquiring knowledge of self.

Having a deeper understanding of what comprises the knowledge of self could provide educators and students with the necessary tools to understand human potential and thus better understand evolutionary psychology—the origin of mental structures—forcing educators to study the power of the mind, drawing from the point of its origin to understand human potential and development. There is much to be gleaned from the Nation of Islam's teaching about the self-creation of God and the evolution of the mind.

Elijah Muhammad declared that when God created himself in the darkness he had no model to pattern from; rather, it was from the creative power of his mind that he was able to create the self: "Think over a man being able to design his own form and he never saw another man before he saw himself" (Hakim, 1997b, p. 273). On the origination of the first life, Farrakhan (2009) adds:

> The Honorable Elijah Muhammad said to us that an atom sparkled in the darkness and God began to create Himself

out of the material of the darkness. He is telling us that matter was there, but the matter was doing nothing. It had no form. It had no aim, it had no purpose, until an atom sparkled in the darkness. (p. 44)

If one were to think of atoms in the sense of ideas, this would mean that in part teachers should be working to stimulate student's ideas. These ideas should then move from a mental vision to the making of a reality that has form, aim, and purpose. Thus, in part, education then serves the purpose of stimulating or awakening the creative mind. With regard to human development, Farrakhan (2009) brilliantly articulates that we must look at the creation of the human being from their origin as a sperm:

Look at you. He said you are "created in His Image and after His Likeness." How did you start from a tiny life germ that impregnated the egg? You can't see it with the naked eye. That is how infinitesimally small that sperm was. But that sperm, with a little tail and a head, had some intelligence in it—it knew where it wanted to go and it knew what it wanted to do. In the dark, that sperm found the egg and the first cell of life began in darkness. But the cell had a light of itself—electricity inside the cell—a neutron, a proton and an electron. The cell of life was like an atom.

The light of itself caused it to start rotating, where it began breaking down and building up. We don't know how long it took for brains to form in the darkness. The first thing that forms when a baby is conceived in the womb is not the tail; the first thing that forms is the head, and it is the head that calls the arms into existence, the feet into existence, and the organs into existence. But when you didn't even have thought, before you could think, there was an intelligence working in you that is The Light of God and The Power of God. Even before the growth of intelligence, in the darkness we were being fashioned

4. Farrakhan and the Human Development Approach to Education

out of a tiny life germ—sperm mixed with ovum; and we were called into existence by what was in the head of that tiny sperm. And at the end of nine months, we came forth knowing nothing, but with a capacity to learn everything. (pp. 44–45)

This has major implications for educators; it informs them that there is a divine essence in the human being that needs to be cultivated. When Minister Farrakhan points out that human beings have the capacity to learn everything, he is providing a reinterpretation of how educators view students, setting up what, in educational jargon, is defined as teacher expectations.

In critical educational theory, this would mean not only making students conscious of existing inequities, but also awakening them to discovering their divine essence. Freire (2000) writes, "people develop their power to perceive critically the way they exist in the world in which they find themselves; they come to see the world not as a static reality, but as reality in process, in transformation" (p. 83).

Newman and Newman (2009) point out that there are domains of consciousness that include the conscious, preconscious, and unconscious processes. The conscious processes make up a small part of the mind and form one's awareness of their current thoughts. Preconscious thoughts can be brought up quickly, allowing one to recall and discuss those thoughts. The unconscious includes those thoughts that are hidden from our view and impact behavior without one knowing it consciously.

Farrakhan has alluded to this when he talks about social engineers skillfully crafting images that impact how Black people, males in particular, see themselves and describing how popular culture has been used as a weapon to depict Black males as a "menace to society." Black youth have internalized these images and have been socially engineered for self-destruction. Freire (2000) observed,

> Submerged in reality, the oppressed cannot perceive clearly the 'order' which serves the interests of the oppressors whose

image they have internalized. Chafing under the restrictions of this order, they often manifest a type of horizontal violence, striking out at their own comrades for the pettiest reasons. (p. 62)

Human development goals are embedded throughout the writings of Farrakhan, especially in his explanation of the Clot. The Clot comes from the Holy Quran, in a verse in the first revealed chapter: "Read in the name of thy Lord who creates—Creates man from a clot." The Clot parallels Elijah Muhammad's idea of the first atom, which sparkled in the darkness, creating motion and time. As the first atom led to the replication of many more, so God thought through the darkness to create a new form of life in humans—and deposited in them the ability to replicate the creativity that brought their own lives into being.

God's ability to think through the darkness is encoded in every human being. He passed on this power to the human family, starting with the original man or the Black man. Farrakhan (2009) posits, "You have so much in you from The Originator, all you need is a proper environment which bring out of you what is in you from The Originator" (p. 48).

For Black people in America, this creative potential was snuffed out by brutality and the slavery experience. The structures against learning and literacy for slaves, was only one aspect of it, as the entire slave experience stripped them of their sense of humanity and, indeed, divinity. For this reason, understanding their personal and also racial past, and being reawakened to their true potential, is the first job of education.

In schools, educators grappling with how to eliminate violence (often gang-related) are too often not taught the deeper reasons behind such behaviors. As a result, educators are not empowered with the knowledge that could free these students from the psychological chains that enslave them. But the writings of Louis Farrakhan can be effective in helping educators understand the role that human development plays in everything from classroom management to school-based violence. Teachers could become more like coaches, working to develop the psychological "muscles" of their students to shed the harmful stereotypes that imprison them and allow their own ideas and creativity to shine.

The Role of Environments in Human Development: Nature vs. Nurture

Educational scholars have long considered the nature versus nurture debate, which centers on whether heredity or environment plays the more significant role in student behaviors and achievement. The nature or hereditarian view argues that heredity is a major factor in determining student achievement. This view has a long history in American life that has been used to subjugate Blacks to second-class citizenship. Hereditarians use IQ scores as the basis for their assumptions and assert that Blacks score considerably lower on these assessments because they are innately inferior to Whites.

The hereditarian view is closely aligned with social Darwinism, which argues that the stronger races survive and the weaker races die off. The historic use of IQ scores to determine intelligence is similar to the modern use of standardized tests to track students. On the history of the eugenics movement, which called upon science to support racist theories, Watkins (2001a) writes, "Scientific racism was a fundamental precept in the architecture of Black education. It was felt that the naturally inferior Black must always occupy a socially subservient position" (p. 40). Using the hard sciences and theology to support White supremacy, these architects formed the foundation of our modern educational system.

The genetic inferiority myth has had a deleterious effect on Black children, who have come to internalize many of these images, making them unconsciously White supremacists as well. The Kenneth and Mamie Clark study of dolls best illustrates this internalized racism that continues to impact Black children. Using White and Black dolls, the researchers asked children questions about racial awareness, racial preference, and self-identification and found that Black children were internalizing negative self-images (Banks, 2006).

Kiri Davis, a female high school student, produced a video titled *A Girl Like Me* (2005), in which a group of Black girls revisit their thinking about Black and White images and, later in the video, conduct with Black children a test similar to the Clark's doll test. During the interview process the Black children compare and contrast the White and Black dolls and answer questions such as: Which doll is pretty? Which doll is smart? Which doll looks like you? Astonishingly, the majority of Black children saw the White dolls in a more positive light than they did the Black dolls.

Schools perpetuate this myth with standardized test results, which they report in newspapers and then later use to decry that something must be done to close the achievement gap. Claude Steele (2004) believed that Black children may actually do poorly on standardized tests as result of what he calls stereotype threat, which occurs when they are being compared to White students.

Farrakhan (2009) indicated how outside influences can distort who we really are: "Environment can influence heredity. We have to be careful what environment we put ourselves in, because no matter what is in you of good, the wrong environment can affect the good that is in you, and turn you into itself" (p. 45). The need to surround Black children with a psychological environment that supports their worth is reflected in the origin history that came out of the Nation of Islam. As Farrakhan (2009) wrote,

> Are you Black because you got cursed? Or are you Black because you took your color out of the darkness from which the First Life came? Since we agree that environment influences heredity, and the darkness before there was sunlight had matter in it that was real, how could the God make Himself up in darkness and come out White? If He made Himself up out of darkness, and the darkness covered Him, then the God Who originated the Heavens and the Earth is a Black God. (p. 45).

Farrakhan is adamant that a major reason Black youth are involved with gang violence is that social engineers have created environments promoting Black self-hatred. The environment orchestrated by these engineers has created behaviors that are contrary to their true selves. For Farrakhan, it is key to replace this false narrative of inferiority with one that reflects the inherent goodness and greatness of Black people. He posits a Black creator God to replace the myth of the White God that dominates American culture. And in later writings he makes clear that it is not one's color that makes one superior but rather one's character and fulfillment of duty to God.

Creativity as a Crucial Component of Development

Newman and Newman (2009) address some significant questions about genetics and human development: "When does an individual's life story begin? At birth? At conception? At the birth of his or her parents or at the birth of their parents?" (p. 84). They assert, "We are each linked back in time, through a life-line comprising our ancestry, our culture, and our genetic makeup" (p. 84). Farrakhan similarly expounds on the individual life story to stress that it originates from the mind of God: "As that first cell of life began rotating in the darkness of the womb, there was light present in it that caused it to rotate" (p. 372).

The act of birth or creation is the first step of all development. And it is the model for all subsequent development as well. When Farrakhan refers to knowledge of God in education, it is partly about learning to unleash in students the creative power that we all have buried inside us. He writes, "God was ever present before anyone had a relationship with you. Your duty is to create, or to make a right relationship with your Creator" (Muhammad, 2006, p. 372). Education is to "lead out or cultivate what Allah (God) has put within so that the world can glorify God by seeing what God has deposited in each human … every human being requires a knowledge of self as part of the proper cultivation of the divinity that is in them" (Farrakhan, 1993, p. 49).

Translated to education, this means that a major component of a proper education involves developing the students' creative mind, which is the divine essence. It is in this area of creativity that schools have failed the masses of youth. In its original definition, school means "a place of leisure." However, developing the creative mind is a threat to corporate interest because it frees individuals to become one with the creator. Farrakhan points out, "Fun is developing the creative mind ... Fun is watching intelligence develop. Fun is feeding intelligence to create the creative mind that the child will be able to say, like God, 'Be,' and it is. That's fun!" (Muhammad, 2006, p. 374).

To cultivate this creativity—the God force within all human beings—the entire scope of education must be changed. Teacher and student expectations change as both become engaged in a process that releases the creative mind, or god power, within. As Farrakhan put it: "You are a wonderful people; you just need a greater knowledge" (p. 63). But the current educational system is not interested in providing knowledge that will lead to power, creativity, or cultivation of the divine essence; rather, it is primarily concerned with mass-producing workers whose labor can be used to reap profit (McLaren, 2015; Spring, 2011).

Even the contemporary schools with their striking new technology are better organized to produce labor in the interest of the ruling elite. Rather than producing authentic thinkers with a high ethical and moral compass, these schools are churning out automatons. Farrakhan (1992) writes:

> We cannot have power without proper knowledge, for it is knowledge properly exercised and implemented that gives us power. Power is the ability to do what we want to do. Power is the ability to remove the impediments that stand in the way of what we want to do. Power is what we need, but we cannot have power until we have the proper knowledge. Knowledge is the perquisite for power. (Retrieved from www.finalcall.columns/mlf-education.html)

It is the hiding of knowledge that has rendered historically marginalized students from ascertaining power. Critical educational theorists highlight that those in power select the body knowledge embedded in school curriculum (Apple, 2004). The psychologists who organize curriculum have put in place bodies of knowledge that do not awaken the divine essence. This is clearly seen in some schools where non-mainstream students are the majority population, especially schools that have predominantly Black students.

The three pillars of education, then, are knowledge, power, and ultimately creativity. Knowledge allows Black students to understand their worth; power allows them to craft an educational system that recognizes their own worth; and creativity is the result of the human development that results from this new educational paradigm—creativity to solve problems, to see new possibilities, to imagine new ways of being and living, and to experience the God-given creative impulse that we are all born with.

Farrakhan on Human Development and Islam

Although Islam has increasingly been associated with intolerance and even terrorism in the American media, it is important to realize that this is a false view of Islam. A good start is the scholars in multicultural education who have devoted entire sections and chapters to the study of Islam (Banks, 2014; Gollnick and Chinn, 2017).

It is equally important for educators to put aside the negative stereotypes about the Nation of Islam (NOI). Although often characterized as divisive and hateful, the NOI has actually sought to uplift Black people, combat the White supremacy that often surrounds them, and allow them to reach their full potential within a culture that seeks to contain and control them.

Gollnick and Chinn (cited in Pitre, 2017) highlighted the positive impact of the Nation of Islam in the Black community: "They often serve as visible neighborhood guardians against crime and drug abuse, and have assumed an important role in the rehabilitation of individuals released from prison" (p. 32). Derrick Bell, a law professor and major contributor to critical race theory, recognized that what is often characterized as hate-mongering in the NOI is simply bringing to light the injustices that surround us:

> Farrakhan ... has decided that the only way to be heard over the racial standing barrier is to place the blame for racism where it belongs. Using language that is direct, blunt, even abrasive, he forthrightly charges those who do evil under the racial structure that protects them and persecutes us, that uplifts them regardless of merit, and downgrades us regardless of worth. If he is sometimes outrageous, who here say that his words are more dangerous or more damaging than the outrages our people constantly suffer? (Delgado and Stefancic, 2005, p. 304)

Bringing Farrakhan's ideas about education to the forefront requires putting aside the tired stereotypes. My earlier work, *The Educational Philosophy of Elijah Muhammad,* was a first step in this direction. According to Elijah Muhammad (1965), the core of Islam is peace: "While teaching and representing a religion called 'Islam' to you, the first important thing to do is to answer the questions: What is Islam? Who is the author? Who are its prophets and people? ... Briefly, 'Islam' means entire submission to the will of Allah (God). It is, moreover, a significant name. Its primary significance is the making of peace, and the idea of 'Peace' is the dominant idea in Islam" (p. 68).

Peace and submission are linked in Islam because submission to God leads to one finding life's true purpose. The purpose of education is to bring one's life purpose to the forefront of consciousness. And it is this new focus on developing the whole person—investing each student with knowledge of his or her power and potential—that is the center of the educational paradigm shift advocated by Farrakhan.

Chapter 5:
Critical Pedagogy

Critical pedagogy is emerging as one of the leading areas of discourse among educational scholars. Nieto and Bode (2012) describe critical pedagogy as a component of multicultural education that empowers educators and students to critically reflect on the political nature of education. Peter McLaren (2015), a leading scholar in critical pedagogy, argues that its major goal is to "empower the powerless and transform existing social inequalities and injustices" (p. 186).

One defining characteristic of critical pedagogy is that it questions how knowledge is constructed; to this end, critical pedagogues contend that those who wield the power in a society determine which knowledge is of most value. By prescribing knowledge these power brokers are able to control and maintain a society that serves their interest while simultaneously making its adherents beings for the state.

In a lecture similar to critical pedagogical discourse, Louis Farrakhan (1993) notes, "he who gives the diameter of your knowledge prescribes the circumference of your activity. If you gain a limited knowledge then you restrict the possibilities of what you can and will achieve" (p. 48). Paulo Freire, considered by some to be a founder of critical pedagogy, examines the relationship between power and knowledge in his powerful book *Pedagogy of the Oppressed*. Freire vehemently argues that the oppressed are perplexed by a plethora of issues that are a result of their oppression. Central to freeing the oppressed is the need to dislodge the oppressor consciousness. In radical discourse, Freire takes aim at the oppressor consciousness, "They are at one and the same time themselves and the oppressor whose consciousness they have internalized"(p. 48).

He argues that the oppressed, "having internalized the image of the oppressor and adopted his guidelines, are fearful of freedom" (p. 47). The scholarly works of critical educational theorists align with Black leaders and scholars who have also questioned the relationship between knowledge and power. Du Bois (1995) similarly argued that Blacks suffered from what he called double consciousness, "one ever feels his twoness—an American, a Negro; two souls, two thoughts, two unreconciled strivings; two warring ideals in one dark body" (p. 45).

Perhaps none have argued as strenuously for the examination of knowledge and power as Elijah Muhammad, Malcolm X, and Louis Farrakhan. The emergence of discourse on the educational achievement of Black students compared with White students has created a need to examine the educational ideology of Black scholars and leaders.

In their book *The Black–White Achievement Gap: Why Closing It Is the Greatest Civil Rights Issue in Our Time*, Paige and Whitty (2010) stress the need for Black leadership to address the educational crisis confronting Black students. Farrakhan has been a major voice of critique and proposed significant statements on the purpose of education, providing the framework to address the education of diverse, but particularly Black students.

A Manufactured Crisis

With the No Child Left Behind Act and Race to the Top taking center stage in the twenty-first century, many continue to express alarm at the achievement levels of Black students compared with White students (Banks, 2014; Giroux, 2015; Ladson-Billings 2009a; Nieto and Bode, 2012). This concern has led many scholars to look for new strategies to address a seemingly unending dilemma. Several have suggested and implemented new programs to help enhance Black

5. Critical Pedagogy

students' achievement levels, while others have conducted research that explores ways to close the achievement gap (Murrell, 2007).

Despite positive efforts that have been made, large numbers of Black children still lag behind White students on standardized test scores. This persistent achievement gap, along with the overrepresentation of Black students in special education classes and other negative variables, seems to subconsciously reinforce what the architects of the "new standards" had intended from the outset: dissemination and internalization of an erroneous belief that Black students are by nature culturally inept and genetically inferior to White students.

Critical race theorists argue that the testing frenzy represents a hidden form of racism that has roots in intelligence tests that were used to label Blacks as being inferior. Ladson-Billings (2009a) writes,

> For critical race theorists, intelligence testing has been a movement to legitimize African American student deficiency under the guise of scientific rationalism ... If the working-class white is "achieving" at a higher level than Blacks, then they feel relatively superior. This allows Whites with real power to exploit both poor Whites and Blacks. Throughout U.S. history, the subordination of Blacks has been built on "scientific" theories (e.g., intelligence testing) that depend on racial stereotypes about Blacks that make their condition appear appropriate. (p. 30)

Upon closer examination one may not clearly see the root cause of underachievement and may therefore miss the opportunity to implement a successful program. The proper questions have not been asked, which has resulted in educators chasing that which is untrue. I use the word "untrue" to demonstrate the ineffectiveness of high-stakes testing as a reliable indicator of student achievement.

Murrell (2007) points out, "The test score discrepancy is a symptom of a much more deeply entrenched system of privilege and educational disenfranchisement that is a major factor in academic underperformance" (p. 4). The standards and high-stakes testing frenzy that has encompassed public schools has created an illusion that has resulted in more punitive and authoritarian policies in majority Black and Latino schools. A majority of schools focus entirely on test scores that are driven by a capitalist, Euro-centered curriculum (McLaren, 2015).

This type of schooling has resulted in Woodson's (1999) term *miseducation* and has affected the education of Black children. The media has seized the opportunity to create a conversation about the achievement gap, but this discussion has not yet raised the proper questions: How do we define achievement for Black students? Is our definition rooted in a Euro-centered version of achievement? Who ultimately shapes this definition and how might it benefit one group and alienate another? Is achievement simply the passing of an exam that has no relevance to critical thinking or problem-posing education?

A definition of achievement is needed to ultimately guide the process that we undertake to reach the goal of education. Critical pedagogues, like Joe Kincheloe (2008), questioned the impact of "official knowledge" on students who have been historically marginalized, observing, "Critical pedagogy mandates that schools don't hurt students—good schools don't blame students for their failures or strip students of the forms of knowledge they bring to the classroom" (p. 13).

The Nation of Islam for over eighty years has a legacy of working with the most downtrodden people in the society and has demonstrated the ability to re-educate those who have been placed on the margins of society. Louis Farrakhan has pointed out the need for "saviors" to emancipate a fallen humanity. In describing love, he declares that at its root are the principles of freedom, justice, and equality. These three principles, when properly adhered to create an environment where human beings live out their purpose and have love for God, others, and themselves. Kincheloe (2008) concurs:

> If critical pedagogy is not injected with a healthy dose of what Freire called "radical love," then it will operate only as a shadow of what it could be. Such love is compassionate, erotic, creative, sensual, and informed. Critical pedagogy uses

5. Critical Pedagogy

it to increase our capacity to love, to bring the power of love to our everyday lives and social institutions, and to rethink reason in a humane and interconnected manner. (p. 3)

The current practice of education keeps students from truly reaching their highest potential, as educators are forced to teach scripted curricula designed to domesticate the creative mind. Nowhere is this more evident than in the current testing regime that has bamboozled educators into chasing a phony version of achievement rooted in the western construction of life and driven by materialistic gain for the few.

Ladson-Billings (2009b) describes this as the "pedagogy of poverty," writing, "There is no place for creativity or real thinking in these classrooms because the only responsibility of the teacher is to prepare students for a barrage of high-stakes standardized tests designed to indicate whether students are worthy of promotion, their teachers worthy of remaining employed, and/or their schools worthy of remaining in operation" (p. 117).

Defining Achievement

Achievement for Black students should be judged by student effectiveness in solving problems and creating new ideas about community building and nation building. Elijah Muhammad writes:

> My people should get an education which will benefit their own people and not an education adding to the "storehouse" of their teacher. We need education, but an education which removes from us the shackles of slavery and servitude. Get an education, but not an education which leaves us in an inferior position and without a future. Get an education, but not an education that leaves us looking to the slave-master for a job. (Muhammad, 1965, p. 39)

Achievement in this type of educational system would be different from the Euro-centered, capitalist-oriented system that serves the purpose of those who rule the society. Under Elijah Muhammad's program, achievement would initiate a process among Backs that would help them take control of their social and educational destiny. Farrakhan (1992) explains the importance of Blacks controlling their own education: "We don't have to ask why we should control our education. The answer is clear. We should control it because if we don't we will always be under somebody else's control" (p. 15).

Carter G. Woodson (1999) asserts that the education of Blacks has been used to control their thinking:

> When you control a man's thinking you do not have to worry about his actions. You do not have to tell him not to stand here or go yonder. He will find his proper place and will stay in it. You do not have to send him to the back door. He will go without being told. In fact, if there is no back door, he will cut one for his special benefit. His education makes it necessary. (p. xii)

Elijah Muhammad (1973) similarly expresses that for Blacks in America, "America's educational system has never benefited you and me, only to keep us a slave to the White man" (p. 96). This speaks to the concept of mis-education. Malcolm X used the analogy of a hunting dog: "Just like a dog who runs out in the woods grabs a rabbit. No matter how hungry the dog is, does he eat it? No; he takes it back and lays it at boss's feet" (Shabazz, 1970, p. 14).

Today's educational system continues to mis-educate too many Black students. Ultimately, educational achievement must be redefined from the perspective of Blacks. Carter G. Woodson (1999) had such in mind when he said,

> The same educational process which inspires and stimulates the oppressor with the thought that he is everything and has accomplished everything worthwhile, depresses and crushes

at the same time the spark of genius in the Negro by making him feel that his race does not amount to much and never will measure up to the standards of other peoples. (p. xii)

Blacks must define educational achievement. They should oppose those in dominant positions who are shaping policies that are negatively impacting them. Freire (2000) affirms, "It would be a contradiction in terms if the oppressors not only defended but actually implemented a liberating education" (p. 54). Elijah Muhammad (1965) critically examines the duality of education that exists between the oppressed and the oppressor, "Certainly the so-called Negroes are being schooled, but is this education the equal of that of their slave masters? No; the so-called Negroes are still begging for equal education" (pp. 44–45).

In defining achievement, we must first begin with who Blacks in America are as a people historically and contemporarily oppressed through education. A careful examination of the slave-making process reveals that it was entirely educational. In what has been argued is a fabrication, the Willie Lynch letter accurately depicts the mindset of those shaping the education of the first Blacks who were made slaves: "Hence, both the horse and the nigger must be broken; that is, break them from one form of mental life to another—keep the body and take the mind" (Hassan-El, 2007, p. 14). These words illustrate both the past and current dilemma in educating Black students. Black education has been controlled by those like Lynch who have crafted an educational agenda that puts to death the creative mind of Black students.

On any given day in some schools, Black students are being advised that they must keep quiet in school and pay close attention. The "good" students are those who can keep quiet and memorize answers. This could be called the *keep quiet syndrome*, and what it really says is that one's thinking and expressions do not matter; what is most important is one's ability to accept the dominant group's way of thinking.

Freire speaks of this when describing the banking process of education, whereby students are merely receptacles into which knowledge is deposited. This process silences students, making them consumers rather than producers of knowledge, and reinforces what happens in the larger society; this is what some refer to as the social reproduction theory. The social reproduction theory contends that schools reproduce within their walls the larger social milieu and its inherent inequalities.

Anyon (1980, 2011), in her work on social class and the hidden curriculum of work, discussed the ways in which schools reproduce what exists in the larger society. Schools that served students in the working class were involved with classroom activities that required rote memorization. These students were being prepared for working-class positions; thus, they were not engaged in critical or creative thinking. Similarly, Black students are less likely to be involved in activities that stimulate critical thinking.

In *Pedagogy of the Oppressed*, Freire (2000) gives excellent examples of how education serves to domesticate oppressed groups. Typically, in these penal-like institutions, some Black students will become more accustomed to the banking model of education that diminishes their critical thinking ability. Freire (2000) wrote that students in oppressive schools will not be asked to think but will be thought of as things. This domestication has been a primary reason for the growing dislike for school among some Black students. Farrakhan (2010) points out, "Gaining knowledge should be a pleasurable experience. When you're in school if it's not pleasurable, who wants to be there? If I am not growing, who wants to be there? If I am not learning something useful, who wants to be there?" (p. 4).

In too many cases, the experiences of Black children reflect those in Farrakhan's 1960 play *A White Man's Heaven Is a Black Man's Hell*. In describing the inequitable and oppressive social condition of Blacks, Farrakhan's musical directly applies to the educational experiences of Black students today. Today the problem of education is that the schooling experiences of historically marginalized students mirror their reality; while for some students, schools are places of joy and happiness, for others they are hellish.

Jonathon Kozol's *Savage Inequalities* cogently describes the schooling experiences of some inner city Black youth: "In Boston, the press referred to areas like these as 'death zones'—a specific reference to the rate of infant death in ghetto neighborhoods—but the feeling of the 'death zone' often seemed to permeate the schools themselves" (cited in Noel, 2012, p. 32). According to Kozol, the schools in his study reflected the communities they were surrounded by, and these communities were places of death.

Unfortunately, the experiences of non-White children, regardless of where they attend school, may prove that schools are indeed "a White man's heaven and a Black man's hell." A visit to predominantly non-White schools reflects these "savage inequalities"; the curriculum is out of touch with the students' life experiences, teachers see their students as culturally deprived, and school leaders develop a school culture that is driven by test scores.

Scholars in multicultural education and critical pedagogy have argued that the curriculum in most schools tends to reflect the experience of European Americans, which leaves a large portion of non-White students on the margins of the learning experience. These scholars contend that knowledge is constructed by those who hold the power positions in the society. What emerges from this knowledge construction is called official knowledge or state-sanctioned knowledge.

Thus, a curriculum is developed that is out of touch with the needs of non-White students. In fact, scholars have argued that what is prescribed in the curriculum actually leads to mis-education. Critical race theorists see the curriculum as a "culturally specific artifact designed to maintain a White supremacist master script" (Ladson-Billings, 2009b, p. 29). Swartz, cited in Ladson-Billings (2009b), writes:

> Master scripting silences the multiple voices and perspectives, primarily legitimizing dominant, white upper-class, male voicings as the "standard" knowledge students need

to know. All other accounts and perspectives are omitted from the master script unless they can be disempowered through misrepresentation. Thus, the content that does not reflect the dominant voice must be brought under control, mastered, and then reshaped before it can become a part of the master script. (p. 29)

A good example of master scripting is the milquetoast image of Dr. Martin Luther King Jr. that is portrayed in textbooks (Nieto and Bode, 2012). More recently Malcolm X has been brought into the master script, making it appear that he had an epiphany regarding white supremacy.

White Man's Heaven Is a Black Man's Hell

Not long ago I visited schools in the Northern United States and was shocked to see how these predominantly White schools allowed children to experience the joy and beauty of education. After attending their first day at one of these schools my daughters, who had been previously schooled in Louisiana, declared elatedly, "Daddy, we are never going back to Louisiana!" When I asked why, they replied, "In this school, we can actually have discussions with other students."

This brought home to me much of the literature on critical educational theory that discusses how White children often experience education in more pleasurable environments. In this particular school, there were no bolted-down chairs arranged in straight lines; rather, students sat at tables or lay on the floor while reading books. The classroom was equipped with a restroom for added student convenience.

The teacher pedagogy was more engaging, allowing students to become active participants in the lesson. The teachers taught students rather than subjects because the students were the subject. There was a *no-homework policy*; rather, parents were encouraged to engage their children in some other learning activities outside of school. School started at 9:00 a.m. rather than 7:45 a.m., so there was never a day that my daughters overslept or had to be pried out of bed. I could see that these students were being turned on to learning, whereas the experience of Black students may be completely opposite.

Both Elijah Muhammad and his student Louis Farrakhan recognized this problem. As a result, they developed an entire system of education within the Nation of Islam to counter the deadening effect of most American education. Farrakhan argues that it is vital that the education of Black students includes the knowledge of self, the knowledge of God, and the knowledge of the time. Knowledge of the time means addressing contemporary concerns in order to propel the student to project his or her thinking into the future. It is through this type of knowledge that students can be "saviors"—teachers—who can change the world.

This perspective explains, in part, why the Nation of Islam so often propounded that separation of the "Black man" is a must. Separation includes a psychological or mental separation from the current world and from the dominant mindset that barraged Black students with messages about their own inferiority. One way or another, separation from the dominant White supremacist ideology would be necessary for students to develop what the NOI called "knowledge of self."

Knowledge of Self and Critical Pedagogy

Farrakhan has argued that the knowledge of self should be at the core of education. Psychoanalytic theory addresses in part the knowledge of self because "it is concerned with underlying assumptions that lie beneath conscious awareness, within discourse and within individual and group behaviors" (Western, 2008, p. 18). In trying to understand how consciousness is shaped, psychoanalytic theory aligns with critical pedagogues who are concerned about critical consciousness.

The Nation of Islam, because of its ability to create a critical consciousness in Blacks that alters their self-concept and thus their group behavior, is persecuted in every circle of leadership. A good example of the psychoanalytic approach and the development of consciousness are scriptural writings that directly relate to the knowledge of self in the Nation of Islam's teaching.

For example, Farrakhan sometimes referenced the New Testament scripture in which Jesus was questioned about when the kingdom of God would come. Jesus replied that the kingdom does not come with careful observation because the kingdom of God is within. This is the basis for the knowledge of self. For Farrakhan, this critical consciousness awakens students to the God power within that is currently asleep or dead. By tasting of the knowledge of self, students' creative minds are brought back to the first creation of life, when the original God self-created himself.

Developing this knowledge of self, causes one to reject White supremacy and allows students to see their true selves, is particularly difficult for Blacks in America. Karenga (2002) notes that of all the immigrants that have come to America, Blacks in America alone were nearly completely stripped of knowledge of the past. They were stripped of their names, their language, their culture, and knowledge of their origins and ancestors. One of the key steps in reclaiming knowledge of self is to reconstruct their history as a people before they were taken to America.

But it goes beyond learning about great African queens, kings, scientists, mathematicians, educators, and so on, though that alone can result in a firestorm of public opposition. It is ultimately about looking back at Black people's relationship to God, in embracing a new narrative about Black people's divine essence to replace the White narrative of inferiority and error. As Naim Akbar (1998) wrote, "The major premise of effective education must be self-knowledge [but] this aspect of the education in self-knowledge creates a serious conflict for the European American educational process" (p. 50).

One must not mistake the knowledge of self to mean simply knowledge of an individual identity but rather one that is tied to a holistic identity that transcends the individual, eventually leading to knowledge of self and others. The idea of self is not a new concept in education; Dewey "insisted that educational experience provided a bridge between 'self' and 'society,' between self-realization and democratization" (Pinar, 2004, p. 17).

The threat to White dominance can be seen in this idea. A true understanding of self in relation to others would help Blacks see what the ruling elite in America has made them. To understand the relationship between the self and others is to resist the political act of mis-education that the ruling elites continue to enforce upon Blacks in America.

Karenga, a leading proponent of Black Studies, has termed what is called Kawaida theory as way of exploring the knowledge of self. Karenga (2002) describes Kawaida theory—the major premise of which could be stated as "Know thyself"—as "a theory of cultural and social change which has as one of its main propositions the contention that the solution to the problems of Black life demand critiques and corrections in seven basic areas of culture" (p. 26).

Those seven areas are the major components of Black studies: history, religion, economics, sociology, politics, creative production, and psychology. Kawaida theory is the knowledge of an individual's past, present, and future possibilities, and understanding these possibilities gives inspiration and motivation, propelling one to tap into his or her creative thinking (Karenga, 2002).

It is an essential component in the process of developing a true self-concept. Karenga notes, "a people whose achievements are minor or whose knowledge of its history and the possibilities it suggests is deficient, develops a self-consciousness of similar characteristics" (p. 70). Education, of course, encompasses all of Kawaida's seven components. Gatto (2002) writes about how to transform education for knowledge of self:

> It is high time we looked backwards to regain an educational philosophy that works. One I particularly like well has been a favorite of the ruling classes of Europe for thousands of years. I use as much of it as I can manage in my own teaching, as much, that is, as I can get away with, given the present institution of compulsory schooling. I think it works just as well for poor children as for rich ones. At the core of this

elite system of education is the belief that self-knowledge is the only basis for true knowledge. (p. 30)

In helping us understand why the knowledge of self has not been implemented for Black children in a majority of public schools, Elijah Muhammad and Paulo Freire provide insight into the purpose and function of White-controlled schools. Elijah Muhammad (1974) directly addresses the purpose of the Euro-centered education in keeping Black creativity from reaching its full potential:

> Our creative thoughts were taken from us until he (the White man) rules his world under his own creative thoughts ... We will be made a new people, for we have been destroyed mentally and physically by the teachers and guides of this world of the White race. Therefore in order to renew us (the once servitude slave and the now free slave of our enemy), we must have a new spirit that will produce ideas in us to become a new people. (pp. 51, 131)

Freire (2000) notes that one of the major issues confronting schools is the technical nature in which they operate. In many cases, the schools are filled with teachers who have no knowledge of the historical reality of their students. He writes that teachers in schools that serve oppressed groups,

> organize a process which already occurs spontaneously, to fill the students by making deposits of information which he or she considers to constitute true knowledge ... Translated into practice, this concept is well suited to the purposes of the oppressors, whose tranquility rests on how well people fit the world that the oppressors have created, and how little they question it. (p. 76)

Schooling thus remains a dictate from the higher-ups that is supposedly designed to make everyone equal. But in believing this myth, the uncritical teacher assumes that the Black student, because of his/her economic status, dress, language, and behavior, has arrived at the point of so-called underachievement because of his or her own shortcomings. This often leads to policies that make schools simply modern plantations, with Black students being held hostage for several hours a day. In the controversy surrounding a Black history program at one school, an issue of major concern for students was the policies designed to keep the students in subjugated spaces, negating praxis (Pitre, 2011).

Freire (2000) provides profound insight into the oppressor consciousness and the oppression that exists in schools: "If they do not have more, it is because they are incompetent and lazy, and worst of all is their unjustifiable ingratitude toward the generous gestures of the dominant class. Precisely because they are ungrateful and envious, the oppressed are regarded as potential enemies who must be watched" (p. 59).

This potential enemy threat has led many schools to have police officers housed on the school grounds. In some schools that are predominantly Black, the police officers and misguided educators resemble plantations with overseers. These negative stereotypes have not only led to oppressive school policies but have played a role in the self-helplessness felt by some Black students.

In some cases, Black students are likely to believe these negative self-concepts and contribute their shortcomings to some fault of their own. Freire describes this as self-depreciation, "which derives from their internalization of the opinion of the oppressors' hold of them. So often they hear they are good for nothing, know nothing and are incapable of learning anything—that they are sick, lazy, and unproductive—that in the end they become convinced of their own unfitness" (p. 63). This might be a major cause for the violence that occurs both in the school and the larger community of Blacks.

Educators have often sought to address the issue of violence by simply looking at the Black students and their community background. There has been no thought about examining the root cause of this violence. A key component to understanding the violence in schools is examining how the oppressed who are shaped in violence display a dual consciousness.

Fanon (1968) notes, "this is the period when the niggers beat each other up" and Freire (2000) asserts that in many cases "to be" is "to be like the oppressor." This often leads to "the destruction of life—their own or that of their oppressed fellows." As a result of not understanding how the oppressed are shaped by historical legacy, they will tend to take out their frustrations on people who look like them, and behave like them.

This attitude is often reflected in the larger community and reinforced in schools where students have no voice. On any given day one can visit rural and urban schools and find Black students in pre-K walking with their hands behind their backs in a straight line to the cafeteria. Once the students are herded into the cafeteria, they are told by their teachers that they must be quiet, or else they will be punished severely. In the classrooms, the same kind of activity takes place under the banking approach of depositing knowledge—educators teach the test rather than the students.

Thus, schools reflect a modern-day Willie Lynch mentality, whereby Black children are indoctrinated to believe that they should keep quiet because their thoughts mean nothing: kill the mind, keep the body. Kincheloe (2008) contends that critical pedagogues raise questions around these issues: "Are teachers merely managers of the predetermined knowledge of dominant culture power?" (p. 5).

What are the possibilities when liberating education mixes with oppressive education? Freire (2000) argues that "sooner or later, these contradictions may lead formerly passive students to turn against their domestication and attempt to domesticate reality" (p. 75). In the final analysis, students will begin to engage in a fight for their liberation:

> Students as they are increasingly posed with problems relating to themselves in the world and with the world, will feel increasingly challenged and obliged to respond to that challenge … Their response to the challenge evokes

new challenges, followed by new understandings, and gradually the students come to regard themselves committed. (p. 81)

Liberatory education is threatening to those with an oppressor consciousness, whose ultimate aim is not to free but enslave. Freire (2000) summarizes the challenge of education for freedom:

> Education as the practice of freedom—as opposed to education as the practice of domination—denies that man is abstract, isolated, independent, and unattached from the world; it also denies that the world exists as a reality apart from the people. Authentic reflection considers neither abstract man nor the world without people, but people in their relations with the world. In these relations consciousness and world are simultaneous: consciousness neither precedes the world nor follows it. (p. 81)

Ultimately, the education of Black students must entail a curriculum that incorporates the knowledge of self to connect students to the disciplines they are studying. Farrakhan (1993) writes, "In the Muhammad University of Islam school system, our students' learning is facilitated because they identify with the subjects. They are taught they are the subjects. They are taught, 'I am chemistry'" (p. 49).

Asante (1991) similarly asserts, "By seeing themselves as the subjects rather than the objects of education—be it the discipline biology, medicine, literature, or social studies—African American students come to see themselves not merely as seekers of knowledge but as integral participants in it" (p. 171). It is easier for students to master the subjects once they realize that each of the disciplines of study is connected to the self.

The Afrocentric Idea

The wave of critical theory that has emerged in the educational discourse has roots in the educational critiques of Black scholars and leaders. In addition, the Afrocentric idea in education offers compelling arguments that are similar to those found in critical theory. Molefi Asante (1991) coined the phrase "the Afrocentric idea in education." Asante examines a concept called centricity, which "refers to a perspective that involves locating students within the context of their own cultural references so that they can relate socially and psychologically to other cultural perspectives" (p. 171).

According to Asante, one of the problems with American education is that "all the experiences discussed in American classrooms are approached from the standpoint of White perspectives in history" (p. 171). He contends that American education is not centric but Eurocentric, meaning that it is grounded in a European perspective. According to Asante, the Afrocentric idea in education has origins in the works of Carter G. Woodson, who critiqued the kind of education Blacks were receiving.

Woodson argued in his book *The Mis-Education of the Negro* that the educational system had what Du Bois called a double consciousness, in that it empowered White students to believe they were superior while simultaneously making Black students feel inferior. Woodson's scathing critique of Black education was particularly concerned with those who controlled what was taught in schools.

As a critical black pedagogue, Woodson (1999) presented compelling arguments regarding Black education: "The education of the Negroes, then, the most important thing in the uplift of the Negro, is almost entirely in the hands of those who have enslaved them and now segregate them" (p. 22). Farrakhan (2006) provides a compelling example, writing, "What books did White people give us to read as children? In kindergarten, we read about Snow White. We read about Goldilocks, even though our locks were not gold. In the first grade, we read about Dick, Jane, and their dog, Spot. We did not look like Dick, nor did we look like Jane" (p. 20).

Farrakhan is not alone in his critique of Black education; there are other educators who are concerned with questions that critical theorists call the selective tradition. Michael Apple (2004), a critical theorist of education, writes regarding the selective tradition, "Whose knowledge is it? Who selected it? Why is it organized and taught this way to this particular group?" (p. 7) Elijah Muhammad (1965) cogently responded to questions about the selective tradition: "we have been to schools where they do not teach us the knowledge of self. We have been to the schools of our slave masters' children. We have been to their schools and gone as far as they allowed us to go" (p. 34).

Louis Farrakhan recalled the Nation of Islam's Lesson Number 1, which asks, "Why does the enemy keep our people illiterate?" (2010, p. 1):

> So he can use them as a tool ... A tool for what? What is a tool? It is an important instrument or utensil held in the hand and used to form shape, fashion; add to, take away from, or otherwise change something by cutting, hitting, digging, or rubbing. But it is also a person used to accomplish another's purposes. He keeps us ignorant so that he may use us as a tool. (pp. 9–10)

Farrakhan's assessment aligns with critical race theorists who argue that Blacks were "real estate" for over 300 years. Ladson-Billings summarizes this relationship, highlighting how race and citizenship intersect. She points out that central to the connection of race and citizenship is the "property issue": "In the early history of the nation only propertied White males enjoyed the franchise. The significance of property ownership as a perquisite to citizenship was tied to the British notion that only people who owned the country, not merely those who lived in it, were eligible to make decision about it" (2009b, p. 25).

Elijah Muhammad addressed this issue in *Message to the Blackman in America*; in a chapter titled "What is Un-American?" He raises questions around land ownership and citizenship, noting the dictionary's definition during that time: "An American according to the dictionary's definition is a citizen of the United States or of the earlier British Colonies; one not belonging to one of the aboriginal races" (p. 183). He goes on to say that this definition "makes clear that (we so-called Negroes) are not and cannot be American citizens" (p. 183).

The education of Black and other oppressed groups has not been left to chance by those ruling society; thus they have shaped the discourse around achievement and removed knowledge of self from the education of the masses. Clearly the knowledge of self, coupled with problem-posing education, provides a powerful platform for stimulating the creative mind.

Problem-posing pedagogy is similar to what some would call the social meliorist theory, whereby students are given contemporary problems that must be solved (Spring, 2006). This approach of solving contemporary problems might make the curriculum more relevant to the needs of Black students. There is also a need to rethink the definition of achievement. The brilliance of Black students is being diminished by the Euro-centered concept of achievement in the same way that success is based on the European concept of rugged individualism.

To effectively bring out the potential in Black children, achievement must go beyond high-stakes testing, disconnected curricula, and other limiting policies set forth in *No Child Left Behind Act* and *Race to the Top*. Ultimately, the education of Black students must be aligned with eternal principles that are rooted in the natural desire for knowledge, helping them to create a new and better world.

Conclusion:
Is There Room in Educational Theory for Louis Farrakhan?

It is safe to say that most people would not think of Louis Farrakhan when they think of educational theory. But the need for a radical change in our educational paradigm has been a core tenet of the Nation of Islam from the beginning. Even newer fields of studies such as critical White studies were first explored by Black leaders such as W. E. B. Du Bois in his classic essay "The Souls of White Folk."

However, over the years, statements made by NOI leaders about Whiteness have been sources of controversy. And these statements are likely to keep educational thinkers like Elijah Muhammad and Louis Farrakhan out of the higher education curricula unless they are understood at a deeper level than they currently are in the popular imagination.

Perhaps the most infamous of these statements is Elijah Muhammad's declaration that "the White man is the devil." This statement has been one of the most heatedly debates statements coming out of the Nation of Islam. It has been interpreted as a simply statement of hate. But what did Elijah Muhammad really mean we he said the White man was the devil?

In part, this statement was a response to the horrors of slavery and racism. Muhammad and others in the NOI had witnessed unspeakable acts of violence and hatred toward Blacks in America. While the racial focus gives the appearance to many that Muhammad and Farrakhan are un-Islamic, their work in America dealt with one of the greatest tragedies in human history. For them, therefore, Islam in America had to first deal with the historical legacy of America's original sins: slavery, White supremacy, and racism. Even more profound, they were dealing with universal White rule that had denied the world's aboriginal peoples their human rights.

But the statement was also an expression of Muhammad's teachings about the origins of race itself. Muhammad taught that the White race was brought into existence from the thought of an original Black scientist by the name of Yakub. As a six-year-old boy playing with two pieces of steel, Yakub realized there were two germs inside of the Black man, and he was ultimately driven to his purpose in life, which was to make a man who was the opposite of the Black man.

This was the White man, whose main characteristic was an inclination to kill those who were non-White. In fact, Elijah Muhammad was talking about a concept called *grafting*, what is currently known as genetic engineering. In defining *devil*, he writes that anything grafted from an original is called devil. For Muhammad, skin color is not the problem; instead, the problem is with characteristics that can be shaped by environment: "This is the main thing. Not that we hate one another's color, the color could be peaceful to us, we have all kinds of colors in the universe to look at, but it is the nature or characteristics of us that we hate, that's the thing" (Hakim, 1993, p. 18).

Scholars of critical white studies have echoed the Nation of Islam's teachings on whiteness. For example, Ignatiev and Garvey (1996) stated that the "key to solving the social problems of our age is to abolish the white race" (p.10). But it is not actual people but rather a mindset, an idea of Whiteness, that needs to be destroyed.

The Nation of Islam's teaching signals the death of White supremacy without the use of physical weapons but instead through the power of the word to create a psychological dilemma for White supremacist ideology. Using the power inherent in a single word—*devil*—they caused an internal psychological struggle for White people that compelled them to examine their actions toward Black persons. If Whites continued to openly lynch, shoot, and murder these people, they would only confirm their identity as the White devil. Perhaps this forced those shaping society to work at hiding those openly White supremacist tendencies that characterized White people as devils. Islam offered White people a chance to escape their nature. It allowed Whiteness to become what Lenardo (2009) called "the center of critique and transformation. It represents the much-neglected anxiety around race" (p. 123), that was slowly being recognized.

It is for these reasons that the educational thought of Louis Farrakhan needs to be recognized in academia. By bringing to the forefront these important meditations on race, educators-in-training can be better prepared to face uncomfortable truths and, as a result, work with vigor toward transforming education in a way that will maximize the potential and development of all children.

References

Akbar, N. (1998). *Know thy self.* Tallahassee, FL: Mind Productions.

Angelis, T. D. (1998). *Louis Farrakhan.* Philadelphia: Chelsea House Publishers.

Anyon, J. (1980). Social class and the hidden curriculum of work. *Journal of Education*, 162: 67–92.

———. (2011). *Marx and education.* New York: Routledge.

Apple, M. (2004). *Ideology and curriculum* (3rd ed.). New York: Routledge.

Asante, M. (1991). The Afrocentric idea in education. *The Journal of Negro Education*, 60: 170–180.

Banks, J. A. (2014). *An introduction to multicultural education* (5th ed.). Boston: Pearson.

———. (2006). *Cultural diversity and education: Foundations, curriculum, and teaching.* Boston, MA: Pearson.

Bell, D. (1992). *Faces at the bottom of the well: The permanence of racism.* New York: Basic Books.

Blount, T. (1994). One postmodern feminist perspective on educational leadership: An aren't I a leader? In S. Maxcy (ed.), *Postmodern school leadership: Meeting the crisis in educational administration* (pp. 47–60). New York: Praeger Publishers.

Bowles, S. (2012). Unequal education and the reproduction of the social division of labor. In J. Noel (ed.), *Sources in multicultural education* (3rd ed., pp. 20–23). New York: McGraw-Hill.

Chomsky, N. (2000). *Chomsky on mis-education.* Lanham, MD: Rowman & Littlefield.

Darder, A. (2002). *Reinventing Paulo Freire*: Boulder, CO: Westview Press.

Davis, K. (2005). *A girl like me* [Film]. Retrieved from http://www.kiridavis.com/index.php?option=com_content&task=view&id=17&Itemid=88888901.

Delgado, R., and J. Stefancic. (2005). *The Derrick Bell reader*. New York: New York University Press.

Dewey, J. (1897). My pedagogic creed. *The School Journal*, 3: 77–80.

Du Bois, W. (1995). *The souls of black folk*. New York: Penguin Group.

Eure, J., and J. Jerome. (1989). *Farrakhan: Back where we belong: Selected speeches by Minister Louis Farrakhan*. Philadelphia: PC International Press.

Fanon, F. (1968). *The wretched of the earth*. New York: Grove Press.

Farrakhan, L. (1960). Retrieved from: https://www.youtube.com/watch?v=cb8xKGaTJhg.

———. (1983). The purpose of knowledge [Speech]. Retrieved from http://www.noi.org/study/knowledge_mlft.htm.

———. (1992). We must control the education of our children [Speech]. Retrieved from www.finalcall.com/columns/mlf-education.html.

———. (1993). *A torchlight for America*. Chicago: Final Call Publishing.

———. (2006). *Education is the key*. Chicago: Final Call Publishing.

———. (2009). *The education challenge: A new educational paradigm for the 21st Century*. Chicago: Final Call Publishing.

———. (2010). Illiteracy: The blight of ignorance on the human family [Speech]. Retrieved from http://www.finalcall.com/artman/publish/Minister_Louis_Farrakhan_9/article_7439.shtml.

———. (2011). God will send saviours [Speech]. Retrieved from http://www.finalcall.com/artman/publish/Minister_Louis_Farrakhan_9/article_7630.shtml.

Final Call (Producer). (2016). Farrakhan speaks: Interview with Alex Jones of INFOWARS {DVD}. Available from https://store.finalcall.com/products/farrakhan-speaks-interview-with-alex-jones-of-infowars?variant=16972706241.

Final Call (Producer). (ND). World friendship tour. {DVD}. Available from https://store.finalcall.com/products/world-friendship-tour-dvd?variant=17394488577.

Freire, P. (2000). *Pedagogy of the oppressed*. New York: Continuum.

Gatto, J. (2002). *Dumbing us down: The hidden curriculum of compulsory schooling.* Gabriola, BC, Canada: New Society Publishers.

Giroux, H. (2015). *Education and the crisis of public values: Challenging the assault on teachers, students and public education* (2nd edition). NY: Peter Lang.

Gollinick, D., and P. Chinn. (2017). *Multicultural education in a pluralistic society and exploring diversity* (10th ed.). New York: Prentice Hall.

Greenleaf, R. (2002). *Servant leadership: A journey into the nature of legitimate power and greatness.* New York: Paulist Press.

Hakim, N. (Ed.). (1993). *History of the Nation of Islam.* Atlanta, GA: Secretarius MEMPS.

Hakim, N. (Ed.). (1997a). *The black stone: The history of Elijah Muhammad.* Maryland Heights, MO: Secretarius MEMPS.

Hakim, N. (Ed). (1997b). *Theology of time (3rd edition).* Atlanta, GA: M.E.M.P.S. Publication.

Handa, M. L. (1986). *Peace paradigm: Transcending liberal and Marxian paradigms.* Paper presented in International Symposium on Science, Technology and Development. New Delhi, India.

Hassan-El, K. (2007). *The Willie Lynch letter and the making of a slave.* Chicago, IL: Lushena Books.

Howard, G. (2006). *We can't teach what we don't know: White teachers in multiracial racial schools.* New York: Teachers College Press.

Ignatiev, N., and J. Garvey. (1996). *Race traitor.* New York: Routledge.

James, G. (2001). *Stolen legacy.* Chicago, IL: African American Images.

Karenga, M. (2002). *Introduction to Black studies* (3rd ed.). Los Angeles: University Sankore.

Kincheloe, J. (2008). *Critical pedagogy primer (2nd edition).* New York: Peter Lang.

King, J. (1991). Dysconscious racism: Ideology, identity, and the mis-education of teachers. *Journal of Negro Education*, 2: 133–146.

Kozol, J. (2012). Savage inequalities: Children in America's schools. In J. Noel (ed.), *Sources in multicultural education* (3rd ed., pp. 30–33). New York: McGraw-Hill.

Kuhn, T. S. (1962). *The structure of scientific revolutions.* Chicago: University of Chicago Press.

Ladson-Billings, G. (2009a). Just what is critical race theory and what's it doing in a nice field like education? In E. Taylor, D. Gillborn, and G. Ladson-Billings (eds.), *Foundations of critical race theory in education* (pp. 17–36). New York: Routledge.

Ladson-Billings. G. (2009b). Race still matters: Critical race theory in education. In M. Apple, W. Au, and L. Gandin (eds.), *The Routledge international handbook of critical education* (pp. 110–123). New York: Routledge.

Lenardo, Z. (2009). Pale/ontology: The status of whiteness in education. In M. Apple, A. Wayne, and L. Gandin, *The Routledge international handbook for critical education* (pp.123–136). New York: Routledge.

Magida, A. (1996). *Prophet of rage: A life of Louis Farrakhan and his nation.* New York: Basic Books.

McKinney, J., and J. Garrison. (1994). The new and improved panopticon. In S. Maxcy (ed.), *Postmodern school leadership meeting the crisis in educational administration* (pp.71–85). New York: Praeger Publishers.

McLaren, P. (2015). *Life in schools: An introduction to critical pedagogy in the foundations of education.* NY: Paradigm Publishers.

Muhammad, E. (1965). *Message to the Blackman in America.* Newport News, VA: United Brother Communication System.

———. (1973). *The fall of America.* Newport News, VA: United Brother Communication System.

———. (1974). *Our savior has arrived.* Chicago, IL: Final Call Publishers.

Muhammad, F. (1993). *The supreme wisdom lessons.* Chicago: IL: Final Call.

Muhammad, H. (2009). *The mis-education of the black educator: Who educates the black educator, and why?* Atlanta, GA: Ratshi Publishing.

Muhammad, J. (2006). *Closing the gap: Inner views of the heart, mind and soul of the honorable minister Louis Farrakhan.* Chicago: Final Call.

Muhammad, T. (1996). *Chronology of Nation of Islam history: Highlights of the honorable minister Louis Farrakhan and the Nation of Islam 1977–1996.* Chicago: Steal Away Creations.

Murrell, P. (2007). *Race, culture and schooling: Identities of achievement in multicultural urban schools.* New York: Taylor and Francis Group.

Newman, P. R., and M. N. Newman. (2009). *Development through life: A psychosocial approach* (10th ed.). Belmont, CA: Wadsworth.

Nieto, S., and P. Bode. (2012). *Affirming diversity: The sociopolitical context of multicultural education* (6th ed.). Boston: Allyn and Bacon.

Noel, J. (2012). *Classic edition sources: Multicultural Education (3rd edition)*. NY: McGraw-Hill.

Orstein, A., Levine, D., and G. Gutek. (2011). *Foundations of education* (11th ed.). Stamford, CT: Wadsworth Publishing.

Ozmon, H., and S. Craver. (2008). *Philosophical foundations of education* (8th ed.). Upper Saddle River, NJ: Pearson.

Paige, R., and E. Whitty. (2010). *The black-white achievement gap: Why closing it is the greatest civil rights issue of our time.* New York: AMACOM.

Person-Lynn, K. (1996). *First word: Black scholars, thinkers, warriors.* New York: Harlem River Press.

Pinar, W. (2004). *What is curriculum theory?* Mahwah, NJ: Lawrence Erlbaum Associates.

Pinar, W., W. Reynolds, P. Slattery, and P. Tubman. (2008). *Understanding curriculum.* New York: Peter Lang.

Pitre, A. (2010). *An introduction to Elijah Muhammad studies: The new educational paradigm.* Lanham, MD: University Press of America.

———. (2011). *Freedom fighters: Struggles instituting black history in k–12 education.* San Francisco, CA: Cognella Academic Publishers.

———. (2015). *The educational philosophy of Elijah Muhammad: Education for a new world* (3rd ed). Lanham, MD: University Press of America.

———. (2017). *Educational leadership and Louis Farrakhan.* Lanham, MD: Rowman and Littlefield.

Purpel, D., and W. McLaurin. (2004). *Reflections on the moral and spiritual crisis in education.* Westport, CT: Bergin and Garvey.

Sagini, M. (1996). *The African and the African American university: A historical and sociological analysis.* Lanham, MD: University Press of America.

Shabazz, B. (1970). *Malcolm X on Afro-American history.* New York: Pathfinder Press.

Shor, I., and P. Freire. (1987). *A pedagogy for liberation: Dialogues on transforming education.* Westport, CT: Bergin and Garvey.

Sleeter, C. (2004). How White teachers construct race. In G. Ladson Billings and D. Gillborn (eds.), *The Routledge Falmer reader in multicultural education* (pp. 163–178). London and New York: Routledge Falmer.

Sleeter, C., and C. Grant. (2009). *Making choices for multicultural education: Five approaches to race, class, and gender* (6th ed.). New York: Wiley Publishers.

Spivey, D. (2007). *Schooling for the new slavery: Black industrial education, 1868–1915.* Trenton, NJ: Africa World Press.

Spring, J. (2006). *American education.* New York: McGraw Hill.

———. (2010). *Deculturalization and the struggle for equality: A brief history of the education of dominated cultures in the United States* (6th ed.). New York: McGraw Hill.

———. (2011). *The politics of American education.* New York: Routledge.

Starratt, R. (2004). *Ethical leadership.* San Francisco, CA: Jossey-Bass.

Steele, C. (2004). Stereotype threat and African American achievement. In T. Perry, C. Steele, and A. G. Hilliard III (eds.), *Young, gifted, and Black: Promoting high achievement among African American students* (pp. 109–130). Boston: Beacon.

Watkins, W. (2001a). *The White architects of Black education: Ideology and power in America 1865–1954.* New York: Teachers College Press.

———. (2001b). Blacks and the curriculum: From accommodation to contestation and beyond. In W. Watkins, J. Lewis, and V. Chou, *Race and education: The roles of history and society in educating African American students* (pp. 40–66). Needham Heights, MA: Allyn and Bacon.

Welsing, F. (1991). *Isis papers: The keys to color.* Chicago, IL: Third World Press.

Western, S. (2008). *Leadership: A critical text.* Thousand Oaks, CA: Sage.

Woodson, C. G. (1999). *The mis-education of the Negro* (11th ed.). Trenton, NJ: First Africa World Press.

Yunus, M. (2007). *Creating a world without poverty: Social business and the future of capitalism.* New York: Public Affairs.

About the Author

Abul Pitre is a professor at Prairie View A&M University in the Department of Educational Leadership and Counseling. He was appointed Edinboro University's first named professor for his outstanding work in African-American education and held the distinguished title of the Carter G. Woodson Professor of Education.

Index

A

Affirming Diversity (Nieto & Bode) 14
A Girl Like Me video (Davis) 48
Akbar, Naim 42
Anyon, Jean 60
Apple, Michael W. 14
Asante, Moleifi Kete 14
A White Mans Heaven is a Black Mans Hell play (Farrakhan) 60

B

Bell, Derrick 52
Bill and Melinda Gates Foundation 26
black children
  black and white doll evaluations 48
  standardized testing shortfall 48
Black males
  classroom suspension rates 43
  depiction as "menace to society" 45
  teacher fears of 16
Bode, Patty 53
Burroughs, Nanny Helen 15

C

Chomsky, Noam 12
Christianity 19, 34, 36
Clark, Kenneth and Mamie 47
critical pedagogy
  achievement level crisis 54, 62
  Afrocentric idea in education 70
  and knowledge of Self 63
  characteristics of 53, 56
  defining achievement 57
  Freire's founding of 53
critical race theory (Bell) 52, 80
Critical White Studies 73

D

Davis, Kiri 48

Dewey, John 33, 64
Du Bois, W. E. B. 54
Dysconsious Racism (King) 14

E

education. *See also* critical pedagogy
  African American achievement levels 54
  Black/Latinx students, labeling of 27
  capitalist-driven focus 56
  challenges in preparing educators 13
  Chomsky's opinion of 12
  Freire on teacher shortcomings 66
  general vs. spiritual view of 12
  Islam's relation to 52
  liberating vs. oppressive 68
  McDonaldization of 12
  miseducation of Blacks 42
  moral/spiritual crisis in 34
  oppressed-oppressor duality 59
  philanthropic contributions to 25
  removal of God from schools 19
Education is the Key (Farrakhan) 33
enslavement of Blacks in America 41

F

Fard, Wallace D. 4, 11

Farrakhan, Louis
  as "prophet of rage" 21
  educational ideas of 30, 34
  educational mission of 11, 20
  lessons from Malcom X 5
  musical talent of 2, 4
  on divine qualities of educators 13
  on origin of first life 43
  Saviors Day convention message 17, 22
Freire, Paulo 14, 45, 60, 66. *See also* critical pedagogy

G

Garvey, Marcus 2, 3
Gatto, John 40, 65
genetic creativity 49
genetic inferiority myth 47
God
  removal of, from schools 19
God Will Send Saviors message (Farrakhan) (2011) 17

H

Hereditarians, use of IQ scores 47
Howard, Gary R. 14
human development
  nature vs. nurture debate 47
  Newman and Newman, theoretical approach 39
  psychological theory of 39
Huxley, Julian 40

I

idealism (philosophical canon) 28
IQ scores
   hereditarian use of 47
   Ladson-Billings opinion of 55
Islam. *See also* Nation of Islam; New Islam
   American view of 51
   Muhammad on meaning of 52
   offer to White people 75
   relation to education 52

J

James, George 30
Jefferson, Thomas 21

K

Karenga, Maulana 64
Kawaida theory (of Karenga) 65
Kincheloe, Joe 56
King, Joyce E. 14
King, Martin Luther, Jr. 62
knowledge of self 11, 43
Kozol, Jonathan 61

L

Ladson-Billings, Gloria 55, 57, 61, 71
liberatory education 69
Life in Schools (McLaren) 14

M

Malcolm X 62
McDonaldization of education 12
McLaren, Peter 14, 53
Men's Only Meeting (on Farrakhan's speaking tour) 16
Message to the Black Man in America (Muhammad) 19, 71
Million Man March 7
Muhammad, Elijah
   message to Black men in U.S. 71
   on aim of education 30, 34
   on duality in education 59
   on meaning of Islam 52
   on missing knowledge of the self 40
   on origin of first life 31, 43
   program for educational achievement 58
   Savior's Day conference lecture 4
   tutelage of Louis Farrakhan 11
My Pedagogic Creed (Dewey) 33

N

Nation of Islam
   charitable work of 56
   difficulties of converts 5
   educational program question 29
   on root knowledge 38
   opposition to Christian teachings 34
   psychosocial/psychoevolution theories and 40

Supreme Wisdom study book 33
teaching of Black-White separation 63
Newman, P. R. and M. N. 39, 49
Nieto, Sonia 14, 53
No Child Left Behind Act (U.S.) (2001) 12, 14, 26, 54

O

Obama, Barack 27
Official Knowledge (Apple) 14

P

Paige, Rod 54
pedagogy of poverty (described by Ladson-Billings) 57
Pedagogy of the Oppressed (Freire) 14, 53, 60
philosophical canons
  idealism 28
  pragmatism 32
  realism 31
Pinar, William F. 14
Pitre, Abut 14
pragmatism (philosophical canon) 32
prophetic dilemma 21
psychosocial evolution theory (Huxley) 40

R

realism (philosophical canon) 31

root knowledge (of Nation of Islam) 38

S

Savage Inequalities (Kozol) 61
Savior's Day convention message 17, 22
scientific racism 47
Sleeter, Christine 14
Social Darwinism 47
Spring, Joel 26, 42
Stolen Legacy (James) 30

T

The Afrocentric Idea in Education (Asante) 14
The Black-White Achievement Gap: Why Closing It Is the Greatest Civil Rights Issue in Our Time (Paige & Whitty) 54
The Educational Philosophy of Elijah Muhammad (Pitre) 14
The Mis-Education of the Negro (Woodson) 14, 70
The Politics of American Education (Spring) 26
The Supreme Wisdom (Muhammad) 33

U

Understanding Curriculum (Pinar, Reynolds, Slattery, Tubman) 18

W

Watkins, W. 47
We Can't Teach What We Don't Know (Howard) 14
Wesling, Francis 19
Western philosophy. *See* philosophical canons
What is Curriculum Theory? (Pinar) 14
White Racism (Sleeter) 14
White supremacist master scripting 61
Whitty, Elaine 54
Woodson, Carter G. 14, 15, 58, 70

CPSIA information can be obtained
at www.ICGtesting.com
Printed in the USA
BVHW040530060222
628089BV00005B/593